On top of old Smoky

Memoirs of an East End childhood to her globetrotting journeys of the sea

by

Brenda J. Coade

Left to right back: Sue, Larry, David, Alan, Bill, Jan, Glad, Diane, Me & Lin
Front: Janet, Mandy & Sally

In loving memory of our brother Bill

Heaven holds a brother who's thought of with much love.
Your charisma a gift of power bestowed divinely from above.
We talk of our memories with much fondness, in time the hurt of your passing will ease and bind us closer together, throughout the remainder of our years.
Brenda

Copyright © 2017 by Brenda Coade

All rights reserved. This book or any portion thereof may not be reproduced or used in any manner whatsoever without the express written permission of the publisher except for the use of brief quotations in a book review.

Published by
Brenda Coade, Great Britain

© Cover artwork by Michael Coade

First edition 2017
ISBN 978-1-5272-1040-0

FORWORD

As you read through this book you will probably notice that I'm a glass half full kind of gal and although I've written a lot about the good times, it does not mean there were not a lot of the not so good times. It's just that I like to think the good times outweigh the bad and that it makes for a more positive reading, as is in my nature. Unlike my husband who ironically is a glass half empty kind of guy and totally my opposite. As they say, opposites attract, but it makes for a rather tempestuous relationship and for the sake of the children we never gave up on it. And as Mike comes from quite an affectionate family, whereas mine are not, he helped me with a lot of help from his late departed mother, to show more love and affection towards my nearest and dearest. Even though at first it seemed quite a hard concept for me because my extreme shyness held me back. And as we had quite an active family life style, I perceived it to be far better to stay together than the alternative of perhaps a part-time father or mother relationship torn apart by our petty squabbling.

ACKNOWLEDGMENTS

Many thanks to my friends Jill whose kind words helped spur me on and Cheryl whose laughter and enthusiasm gave me the confidence to finish the book and for giving it a final proofread.

A special thank you also to my sister Linda for her love, understanding and patience and who in her spare time helped me with my dictation, the books layout and structure and also proofreading the book.

Another huge thank you to my wonderful son Michael, who I love so very much, for his understanding and patience whilst helping me write, and for the fantastic art and design work on the front cover of this book.

And last but not least my dearest daughter Zoë who I love more than words can say, for her design and publishing skills that made it possible to turn this story into an actual book.

POEM

As we lay protected under a makeshift billowing sail,
Snug in our wetsuits from the elements all around.
We ate our fill after our dive in the deep,
Then scoured our islands seaweed strewn heap.
Seashell and starfish shimmered in pristine white sand,
Basking and half backed in this far off wonderland.
Lost under a blanket at twilight to a coral blue sea,
Over hung by a star-studded sky in a night canopy.
At sun rise our footprints will cease to explore,
So for now you sleep silently in your watery grave as afore.

Brenda Coade

PART ONE

CHAPTERS
The Swaby Family
Dad
Mum
Mum's Illness
Larry
'Uncle' John
Nanny-Pots
Grandad Jamie Waite
Maplin Street & Nanny-Pots Garden
Nanny –Pots & George in Bethnal Green
School – and Delores!
Brokesley Street and Things That
Go Bump in the Night
Who's that creeping about?
Memories of Growing-up in Mile End
Fred and Mary
My Sister Gladys
Folk Healing
Story-telling
Coborn Road – More Things That Go Bump…
My Sister Linda
Christmas Revels
Mum's Sister, Nance
Phoenix School

PART TWO

CHAPTERS
Marriage to Michael Coade
Harold Hill
Michael and Zoë
End Note

PART THREE

CHAPTERS

Scuba Diving - Trainee Diver
Fort Bovisand
My first holiday to the Red Sea
Sea-houses
The Chris Christianson and the SS Somali
The Riversdale, Salcombe
Lundy Island and the Carmen Filomena
Shoreham – Looe Gate Reef and the Stanoola
Puerto Del Carmen – Red Cross Reef
The Maldives
Baltimore – The Kowloon Bridge
Eilat – The Sateen, and Taba
La Cave des Tuileries
Le Lavandou, Southern France
Port de Tort and the Spahis
Cherbourg – The Strathblane and SS Ousso
Normandy – Omaha Beach, the Empire Broadsword, the USS Susan B and the Anthony LST 527
HMS Sesame, the USS Meredith, and the Sora
Deafness
Australia – Hong Kong
Australia – Cairns and the Taka 2

The Maureen of Dart
The Edison and Wolf Rock Lighthouses, The Hathor, The Plympton, The Cita, The Maine and The Manacles
The Oban, Scotland – The SS Breda, The Tapti, The Hispania and The Port Napier
The Kylebarn, Jim and Sandy
Sandy
Tanzania
Mafia Lodge
Mafia Island
VIPs at the Hospital on Mafia Island
The Red Sea, Egypt
The Thistlegorm
Shark Reef and the Yolanda
The Elphinstone Reef
East, west, the Red Sea's the best!
Dolphins
Return to the Maldives
The Northern Atoll, The Villingili Kanda Reef
Kuda Kandu
Why Do I Love Diving?

In closing,

PART ONE

The Swaby Family

As far back as I can remember, my childhood years were plagued by unresolved things going BUMP in the night! Or maybe, it was just that I was more sensitive than my siblings. I was born in East London, on the 25th July 1951, at the Mile End Hospital in Bancroft Road, a true cockney by all accounts.

I was named Brenda Joyce – Joyce after my godmother. I am the sixth child in the middle of what was to become a family of twelve – four boys and eight girls. We all had nicknames, not necessarily just diminutives of our proper names; starting from the eldest: Linda Mae, called Lin or Lou-lou; Gladys Ann – Poggles; William Robert – Billy or Bangers; Alan Frederick James – Moogie; Susan Elizabeth Mary – Suky or Witch; myself – Gabby or Crummy; David George – Dai Bach; Diana Rose – Mingie; Laurence Frank – Guv; Janet Elaine – Wormy; Amanda Kathleen – Mandy; Sarah Ann - Sally.

My own nickname, Gabby, seems ironic as I was painfully shy. But it was the corruption of an affectionate little nonsense rhyme that my mother sang as she danced me on her knee "Brennie, Brennie, from Abergavenny." My siblings' attempts at Abergavenny resulted in Gabbygavenny, thus Gabby. I would often hide away from visitors, where under the table amongst the cake crumbs was a favourite. As Mum served her visitors with tea and cake, she would hand small morsels of cake down to me – hence Crummy!

Dad

Dad, Robert Walter Swaby, was born in 1925 in Poplar, East London. Fair-haired at about 5ft.8in tall he was a quiet man by nature, but not one to upset, either. He was known as Bob, the local handyman, and always looked ready to get down to some hard work! He wore his shirts sleeves neatly rolled back to his well-defined biceps, with his shirt (and jumper in winter!) tucked deeply into his old khaki army issue trousers, all held in place with a thick, black leather belt that fitted snugly around his trim waist. Not unlike Harry H. Corbett in the TV series Steptoe & Son!

But with his steely grey/blue eyes, slim features, 'designer stubble' and permanent cigarette-butt constantly on the go, I thought he was more Clint Eastwood than Steptoe. He was also a bit of a ladies' man, by all accounts; with supposedly more offspring whose conception coincided with the time he spent on exercises into France with the Army.

He was just as tough as Clint, too. He rarely spoke of his time in the Armed Services, but the family legend was that he was blown up in France and woke up in hospital stone deaf and unable to speak. From the name Swaby, which is of German/Dutch origin, on his mangled dog tag, they assumed he was German. It wasn't until he was seen by an English-speaking doctor, trying to make sign language gestures to a nurse, that it was realised he was English and he was relocated to a hospital back home. I dread to think what could have happened to him otherwise – sent to a German hospital in Germany, or even a prisoner-of-war Camp. Although his powers of speech and some hearing eventually returned, he remained hard of hearing for the rest of his life.

When we were quite small, he helped Mum to look after us whenever possible. He was quite a good cook, learned from his spud-bashing days in the Army, no doubt. He could turn out a nice Sunday roast with all the trimmings.

He tried his hand at selling ice-cream once, pedalling around on a tricycle with a big refrigerated ice-box on the front. He didn't last long, though, as he kept giving his stock away. Fortunately he was quite resourceful, and had his handyman / painter / decorator skills to fall back on, between casual jobs.

He learned his skills by trial and error mainly as there was always plenty to make, repair or paint over in our house and his skills and reliability were common knowledge in the neighbourhood. Later, when we moved house, our new neighbour's son, Mr. Levy, was a professional interior decorator. He often employed Dad on a casual basis at weekends, to do some of the more mundane tasks. Dad gained some valuable professional expertise in this way. On several occasions, he also took me along to make tea and to help clear some of the bigger houses, such as those in Richmond and other similar places. Some of these experiences must have rubbed off on me, as I quite enjoy doing home decoration.

Sometime later, Dad got a job in Barton's Cooperage as an apprentice cooper. He completed his indentures and worked there for many years, working his way up to charge-hand. He tried to introduce my brother Billy into the industry, but it was tough, dirty work and not for Bill.

Every morning at about eight o'clock, just before waking everyone else up, he would make himself several jam sandwiches for lunch, packed neatly into yesterday's bread wrapper, to fit into his overcoat pocket. In the winter months, you would often find him balanced on one foot, with the other propped up on the top of the oven door, warming his feet and socks before tucking them into his old-fashioned hob-nail boots – another remnant of his army days. With a still-smouldering cigarette-butt tucked behind his ear, he would finish his breakfast of a mug of tea and a folded over slice of bread and jam.

After taking Mum a cup of tea, he would kiss her goodbye – something he never forgot to do. Before retrieving his big old, army coat from the bed; placed there for the dual purpose of keeping them warm and also to pre-warm it before putting it on. Just before leaving the house he'd place his flat cap snugly over his fast-receding head of once fair curls, ready for the journey to work. When he had the cash for all the 'legal' necessities – bell, dynamo-driven front and back lights, cycle-clips and pump, he used his old cycle. If any of these requirements were missing, then he would walk a brisk half-hour to the Cooperage at Stratford.

I believe he loved that job, though. Alan once told me that one of the perks of Dad's job was the dark, sticky tar-like alcoholic deposits scraped and drained from the bottoms of the old oak barrels he was now employed to deconstruct or renovate. This black, potent fermentation was said to be 100% proof. He stored it in an old 'Bev' bottle, which once resulted in it being used as instant coffee – much to the disgust of the drinker, and the annoyance of my father at the waste of his hoard. It probably kept him sane, as a drink down at the local was a luxury he could not afford. Eventually, a combination of the demise of the cooperage industry and his failing health resulted in his early retirement.

Although rarely ill as a young man, despite his Army experiences and being a heavy smoker, he had developed severe lung problems. On the advice of his Doctors, he managed to give up smoking, which probably prolonged his life for a further four to five years.

I have fond memories of him, back home from one of his frequent stays in hospital. He was standing at the half-open back door in the kitchen, saying how good he felt whilst breathing in the fresh air and warming himself in the rays of the spring sunshine that streamed in through the door opening. It was nice to see him standing there happy and contented; even if it was to prove the last time he came home. For some time now he had been unable to stand for any length of time and relied heavily on his Nebuliser to help him with his breathing.

During one of his low moments, which occurred when he had to return for what was his last hospital stay, I got a glimpse of the regrets he felt for the way his life had turned out. The ward was like any of the countless others he had been in that year, with a cleanliness that left you cold. As I stood at the bottom of his bed, I noticed his perfectly manicured nails against the perfectly folded sheets. He had been in and out of hospital so many times it was as if he were a part of that sterile environment, rather than the reality of the grime and toil of his working life.

"Do you think," he said with a little sadness in his voice, "we would have had a better life if we had gone to live in Canada?"

"I don't think our life would have been much different from what it is now," I said. "You would probably have ended up cutting wood in a saw-mill much the same."

I recall there was a government recruitment drive on in the sixties or seventies, for strong men with all sorts of manual skills and with bigger families to immigrate to Canada, with offers of subsidised fares. I think Dad thought that the emphysema, which was slowly killing him was probably worsened by the inhalation of the dust from the sawn wood he worked with as a cooper, might have been avoided if we had emigrated. Also, Mum would have loved to have gone back to her native Canada, where she was born. But Dad had had reservations, so he did not pursue it. I believe he deeply regretted it at the end of his life. He died in 1989, aged only 64 years, from pneumonia and complications brought on by emphysema.

Mum

Dad had met Mum, Ilo Mae Isobel Waite, when they were about fifteen years old at the local biscuit factory where they both worked alongside Mum's sister Shirley (called Nance). Also working there was John, who much later came to live with us when he lost his house. Out of respect we always showed to adults, he was called 'Uncle John', even though he was not a relation.

Mae, as she preferred to be known, was born in Ontario, Canada, in 1924. She was named after her godmother, a full-blooded Native American Indian of the first nations Cree, who lived in a tepee on the reservation near my grandfather's ranch.
It was there mum was given the unusual name of Ilo, meaning either 'star' or 'chief's daughter' according to who was telling the story. She often told us stories of the 3 mile trek she and Uncle George had to endure to get to school, the deep snow-covered valleys, the hot summers, and the tumbling grasses of the wide prairie land, around the farmhouse where she was brought up. Her father Jamie Waite was given the name Coyote probably by the Cree, died in 1936, and was buried in his own twenty acre wood. My great grandfather a half blood was possibly of the first nations Cree. But his father my great great grandfather was thought to be of Micmac origin.
In 1938 my widowed grandmother, Nanny-Pots brought her family back to England when mum was about fourteen.

Standing about 5ft.3in tall, she was an attractive, well-rounded woman, with a merry, open face and blue eyes. Her hair was dark, and she wore it fairly long, rolled back from her face and resting in loose curls on her collar, as was the fashion in the forties. She reminded me of the looks and stature of our Queen, not like me, fair skinned, tall and gangly.
She was quite placid by nature, rarely getting angry. I only once saw her and Dad having a bad argument, which lasted about 24

hours, and I remember that it upset me badly at the time. She'd tell you off before resorting to a smack – usually a sharp slap across the backs of the legs. That was usually enough to stop you in your tracks, whether she used her hand or the occasional slipper. As we got older and probably more unruly, she would grab a garden cane, which stung like heck. And if my brothers were extremely naughty, she would tell Dad and he would take his belt to the boys' backsides. It could be quite frightening sometimes, especially if he lost his temper. You'd see him unfasten his belt in frustration and chase my brothers around the house, with steam coming out of his ears. It didn't happen very often, though, and he would be easily calmed down, so thankfully there was never any real injury.

The early years of her marriage were taken up with having babies, bringing up children, washing and shopping. I think she must have detested housework, because she had great difficulty keeping on top of the cleaning, despite the help we all were required to give. It's something I find quite rewarding myself, probably because of the early training. Despite all our best efforts, though, it was a never-ending task to keep the house clean and tidy. So sometimes, to escape the humdrum of constant washing and cleaning, she would down tools and declare a 'Baking Day'. She was good at baking and passed a lot of her recipes on to us girls. Many of them were her own inventions, based on favourite cakes but reflecting her need for economy.

On 'Baking Days', she would make half-a-dozen or so of the most delicious pies and cakes: lemon meringue pie, sultana meringue pie and one of my all-time favourites, Queens Pudding. Mum's version was a pastry-lined dish, filled with a layer of thick-cut bread, buttered and jammed, then covered in custard and desiccated coconut. This was baked, and then left for the custard to 'set'. As we ploughed our way through so many loaves of bread in a week, bread and jam being a stable meal, there were always odds and ends of a loaf and she used these up to produce huge, sweet, spicy bread-puddings. These were always useful, too, to butter up the rent-man if she was a bit short on the rent that week. It's no wonder I have such a sweet tooth.

When we moved to Coborn Road, Mum regained a little of her independence and got herself a job. She worked hard throughout the week, sometimes into the late evening. At one stage she was juggling three part-time jobs. We saw little of her during the week, but there was always a cooked meal waiting in the oven for us when we got home. As Sue got older, she took over the cooking of the evening meal in return for a little pocket money and I would help with the clearing up and cleaning the kitchen. Sometimes, Mum would reward me with a little present from the market, which infuriated Sue as she said it made her feel like a paid skivvy!

Mum (called May by her friends and neighbours) had a natural zest for life and a great sense of occasion. She never missed the opportunity to party – weddings, christenings, Christmas, Easter, birthdays, any festive occasion would see a huge gathering of friends, family and neighbours at our home, followed by a big 'blow out' of home-cooked food and goodies. With her open friendliness, she was a popular figure. Her very good friend, Val, lived a little way up the same road as us. Her son, Young Jimmy, was my brother Laurence's best friend. Val was a jolly woman, a larger, fair-haired version of Mum. Val also had a big family, and they found they had a lot in common. Val's family was as big as ours, but nothing seemed to faze her and she always seemed to be laughing or joking about something or the other. They soon became firm friends and got a job together in the local mirror factory, J & H Brown, under the railway arches at the end of Coborn Road. .They worked on big pressing machines, pressing out plastic face powder compacts and hair-brush sets. As young kids, we had great fun under the arches, racing down the hill with one skate each. My brothers used the hill to race their home-made carts, fashioned from an old pram chassis and wheels, with an orange-box fastened on top and string steering tied to the wheelbase.

Val's husband, Big Jimmy, was a tall, large, no-nonsense man with dark unruly hair like Ken Dodd's. He kept himself very much to himself, except when it came to showing off his model railway. It was probably the biggest model railway in the whole of East London. It covered the entire attic floor, set up on two levels so that the trains could go under each other through different tunnels. The track wound past little streets full of model houses with painstakingly painted brickwork and tiny trees in different shades of green. On the platform at the station, crowds of little people waited in various poses for the train to arrive. On rare occasions he would invite us to look around the layout, provided we did not touch it. He took great delight in demonstrating how the signals worked and how the lines moved the train from one track to another, whilst blowing his whistle, dressed in his signalman's hat and jacket. It was a great shame that he did not live beyond forty years.

Whenever Mum worked on the late shift, Dad would drive up to the factory in his lime-green Ford Anglia to collect her. Sometimes, on a Friday 'pay-day' they would bring back a big parcel of fish and chips for our suppers. Sometimes, if she had had a good week, they would bring a Chinese take-away. We would then all sit around the TV, to watch the late-night horror movie. We balanced our take-away on our knees, eating them straight from their wrappers or containers, to save on the washing up. Occasionally, on a Sunday, the wet fish man came down the street and we would be treated to smoked haddock with bread and butter.

Mum and Dad were offered a large, brand new maisonette in Grove Road, about a quarter-mile away from Coborn Road, which was due to be demolished. She obtained a job as an early morning cleaner in the Bank of England, in Threadneedle Street, London. She worked her way up to being part of a team setting up official functions. In this capacity, she was introduced to many influential people, including Government officials and Royalty. We still have a souvenir plan of the place settings and a signed letter of thanks from Mrs Thatcher after one of the many banquets Mum helped to arrange.

Mum was also invited to one of the Queen's famous garden parties. The invitation included one guest, so Mum took Linda. Lin, our oldest sister, was one of the more studious in the family, staying on at school and going on to college. She had done a little modelling, before becoming a personal assistant in a publishing company. She later went to Teacher Training College and became a teacher, completing her teaching career as the Deputy Head of a school for children with learning difficulties. On this occasion she was the perfect companion for Mum, with her good dress sense and articulate manner

Mum's Illness

Now Mum had more time to garden and she filled the large front garden of her new maisonette with pretty flowers and shrubs. She tended to them with love and pride and it was admired by all who passed by. There was a bus stop outside Mum's front gate; so, the people queuing and the passengers on the bus would admire her handiwork.

Mum, too, enjoyed quite good health, despite having given birth to twelve live babies. So when she began to feel and look quite jaundiced, she dismissed it as side effects from some dodgy seafood. We eventually prevailed upon her to go to the doctor, where she was diagnosed with Hepatitis B. She received a very stern letter from the hospital about personal hygiene and was required to inform all her friends and contacts, about her condition, in order that they could arrange to be vaccinated. She felt like a leper. Some people got themselves checked out and vaccinated, others didn't bother. I didn't because I could not believe the diagnosis. Several likely scenarios were given to her, including dirty beer glasses at the pub next door, but she rarely drank. And if it were that contagious, how come no-one else had 'caught' it from her, despite her being ill for some time? However, she lost a few friends at that time and had to give up her beloved job at the Bank.

However, when her condition did not improve she underwent further examinations and it was eventually discovered that she had, in fact, cancer of the bile duct. Because of the type, and site of the cancer, both surgery and chemotherapy were ruled out in favour of a new less invasive treatment. This required frequent visits to hospital to insert and then monitor various 'stents' to by-pass the cancerous organ and drain the bile from her body.

A couple of weekends before she died, I left my family at home and went to sleepover with her at the maisonette. It was fairly easy for me to spend the weekend with her if she needed someone at short notice and no-one else was available. All the girls had by this time left home to bring up their own families, but all took the time to care for Mum. Looking back, I feel I was privileged to spend this time with her, getting to know her a little better.

The pain-killing drugs she took also left her incontinent where at night she often needed someone to help clean and dress her after an 'accident'. She found this a little strange and uncomfortable, as she was a fairly private person – you rarely saw her undressed and in her nightclothes except when she was hospitalized. I particularly remember one night, when she needed to go to the bathroom. Not wanting to wake me again, she tried to get out of bed on her own, but fell, and could not pick herself up again. I heard her fall, and ran to lift her, pulling her up by the arms. I was totally unsuccessful, and we just ended in a heap on the floor, crying in fits of uncontrollable laughter. In the end, we decided we would have to enlist the aid of Larry, who still lived at home, to help pick her up. She thought it was undignified for her youngest son to see her in her nightie, but we really had no choice.

Larry

Larry was a strong, stocky young man, with straight hair and Jon Bon Jovi looks. He was quite a shy man, not very articulate, and dyslexic, but a very talented artist. He loved to draw giant cartoon pictures and if he couldn't find his sketch pads he drew on his bedroom walls and anywhere else that wasn't moving. He was once offered a job with one of the daily newspapers in the cartoon department but, because of his shyness, he turned it down. We all thought it a great shame because it might have helped to bring him out of his shell. He found a way to use his artistic talents, though; working in a tattoo studio after the lady owner spotted his talent. He had taken a cartoon he had drawn into the studio to ask for it to be made into a tattoo. He was invited to bring back more of his collection of pictures and she was so impressed with his art-work that she helped him to apply for a course in tattooing, with the promise of a job at the end of it..

Towards the end or her life, Mum had great difficulty breathing when she was lying down, so I used to prop her pillows up until she was almost in a sitting position and then we talked throughout the night. She told me she was not afraid of dying, but was frightened of the pain. I thought she was very brave and could not believe she was dying. She had been such a strong woman, both physically and mentally, but two years of pain had left her exhausted and half her pre-illness weight of fifteen stone. She seemed to know that she could not make it through many more pain-filled nights.

When Lin arrived the next day, she asked to be taken to the hospital. The doctor told Lin they would admit her to hospital, awaiting transfer to the local hospice. He gave her a fortnight to live, at most. Lin contacted Alan, who spent the rest of the day and half the night, too, contacting all the family and all those people he thought would like to come to see her for possibly the last time. By about nine-o'clock that evening, Mum was delirious, appearing to hallucinate, saying things like "Look at the nice white carpet around the bed" – it was a dark-brown varnished floor. Then she said that the smoke from the barbeque would make all those pigeons' feathers dirty if they don't fly away'. Then she really scared me by asking me not to forget to order the flowers in the morning. My mind was in turmoil; did she know she was going to die? She tried to put a brave face on it and, despite being in obvious pain, refused to take the painkillers and sleeping tablets whilst we were all there. So we made the painful decision to all go and leave her, so that she could take her pills and sleep. I think that in our hearts we all knew that this was the last time we would see her alive, and we were told by the nurses that as soon as we had all gone, she had gone to sleep, without taking her medication and died in her sleep in the early hours, from the liver cancer. She had lived for two years from the initial diagnosis of cancer of the bile duct and we were later told that it was the longest anyone had lived so far with this condition and treatment.

Next day, Lin, Bill and I went back to the hospital to verify her death. I had decided that I would not see her body, preferring to remember her the way she was. Lin formally identified her, and at the last moment I changed my mind and went into the cubicle where she lay. I couldn't face never having the chance to see her again. In some ways, I do regret changing my mind, because where she had been lying in the foetal position, her face and body were all blue down one side, like a big bruise, caused, the nurses said, by the blood being starved of oxygen. I try not to dwell on it, and to remember her when she was so alive. At least she died in her sleep and was out of the frightening pain she had to endure. I've come to terms with it now and I think all the good times outweighed the bad, which is why I feel compelled to share them in my story.

My one big regret is that I was not able to take her back to Canada before she died. We had planned to do it when I had the chance and while she was in remission after having radiotherapy. On reflection, the planning probably helped her to cope with her condition as she had something to look forward to. Whenever you visited her, she would bring out her suitcase and show you the new clothes she had bought and packed, ready for the trip. Sorry, Mum.

'Uncle' John

Uncle John was not in fact a relation, but had worked in the same factory where Dad had met Mum. Alan told me of the time he and Bill were playing truant and they met John. He pulled them up in the street, saying:
"You're the Swaby boy's, aren't you?"
One of them replied cheekily "Who wants to know?" and John replied that he was the Schoolboard Inspector. Billy and Alan knew that they would be in for a hiding from Dad's belt once he knew they had truanted, but when they got home nothing was said. So they thought they had got away with it. Imagine their horror a couple of months later when John turned up on the doorstep. They thought he would surely mention the incident, but luckily for them John never said a word.

After Dad died, Uncle John, who had lived with us on and off for about twenty years, was of enormous help to Mum, especially in her last years when she was very ill. He shopped, cleaned, cooked and helped her run the household. Short, dark and stocky in his habitual sleeveless pullovers, he had something of the ruggedness of Jack Palance. He was a labourer, working at the Docks or wherever he could get labouring work. Although a good worker, he wasn't at all ambitious (probably because he was almost illiterate) and was a bit too fond of a drink or two or four. When we were young, he was good at helping to look after us – in my opinion he would have made a good nanny. He was patient and kindly, and ensured that we had our baths, and had our clean clothes ready for school.

His fondness for the drink had led to his mother not allowing him to come in when he arrived home drunk, so initially he came to us to spend the night on the sofa 'sleeping it off'. After his Mother's death, he came to live with us almost permanently, and with so many children it was good to have another pair of hands.

Nanny-Pots

Mum's Mother, Mrs. Edith Emily Waite (Nanny-Pots) as she was sometimes referred to because of her love of gardening, lived a few streets along from us, at the top of Maplin Street, near Mile End Station. Our 'Nanny-Pots' was a proud and upright lady, who appeared taller than her 5ft.4in. Her hair was usually held in a large net-covered 'bun' on top of her head, and she had kindly blue eyes. The rolls beneath her double chin bulged down in layers over the collars of the neat, navy, nurse-style dresses and blouse and skirt outfits she liked to wear, often topped by the brightly coloured floral wrap-around 'pinnies' that tie at the back in a bow. In cold or wet weather she wore a long, navy, double-breasted coat, almost to her feet. She favoured elegant, flapper-style strap-over shoes, with low shapely heels – we knew them as 'Nationals'. A small black hat, trimmed with red cherries covered in back netting, was secured to her head with a long, pearl-topped hatpin. This made her look kind of fore-boding and stern, more like a nursing sister than the chain-smoking, flower-loving, dearly loved grandmother who she actually was.

She never liked to see her reflection in a mirror, because she didn't like the fact that she was getting old. She had the most wonderfully soft skin and fresh complexion, due I think to her habit of wiping her face with the inside of the cucumber skin when making a sandwich. It's very effective at cooling you down on a hot summer's day. This is something I always do too; as we now know that fruit acids help to smooth skin and soften wrinkles. Her long grey hair, usually severely wound back in a bun, was left long and loose at home, revealing a yellow nicotine streak across the front, the result of her chain-smoking habit. She started smoking when she was about sixty, she said to help her nerves and progressed to forty or more Woodbines a day. She had the most unusual way of smoking, impaling the cigarette onto the end of the pearl-topped hatpin and then just puffed at it.

I don't think she ever inhaled the smoke properly it just rose around her in a constant, thick blue swirl. Her family, the Loveseys, were from Berkshire and that is where she was born. I think her father was a landowner and the family were quite well-to-do.

Grandad Jamie Waite

She was swept off her feet by Granddad, Jamie Waite, with his tales of ranch-style living back home in Ontario, Canada. So she married him and immigrated to Canada, where she raised a large family, plus a couple of abandoned 'foundlings' presumable left on their doorstep by the Cree Indians living on the reservation near buy.

Until one bitterly cold winter's day in 1936, when huge snowdrifts had covered the house, Grandad needed to go outside to the stores for fuel and provisions to stock up. He didn't return. When after several days the blizzard conditions eased off, he was found frozen to death, still on the roof-top, sitting propped up against the chimney stack which doubled as the emergency escape route in extreme conditions.

Maplin Street and Nanny-Pot's Garden

In 1938 Nanny sold up and returned to England. She lived in London, where she taught piano for a time. After the war, she lived with Uncle George, Mum's last surviving brother, in a tiny terraced cottage that used to be a part of the grocery store next door.
The green front door to the cottage was very low, with a big black door knocker and a small bottle pane glass window. The letterbox was halfway down, so you had to stoop to shout through it if Nanny was in the garden and couldn't hear the knocker. Looking through the bottle glass window distorted everything inside and the sunlight reflected on the hallway made nice rainbow patterns on the lead-painted wooden panelled walls.

In the front room, which Nanny called the front parlour, the now redundant display window of the old shop front stretched across the entire length of the living room. It was dressed with beautifully hung lace and net curtains and always seemed light and sunny in there, even on the dullest of days.

In one corner stood an upright piano, covered with a beautiful hand-crocheted runner to protect the wood. When you opened the lid, the words 'Steinway' in large gold letters were emblazoned inside. A twisted barley-leg stool covered in a dark green tapestry cover was tucked beneath. A highly polished silver cake-stand, you could see your reflection in it, stood on top of the piano, in the middle. A set of crystal cut-glass fruit or jelly bowls were set to the side, with a punch-bowl set, probably made from crystal too, sat at the other side. The little cups that hung from the punch-bowl swung to and fro as you opened the parlour door and a rainbow of twinkling lights danced all over the walls and furniture, filling the room with reflected sunlight.
Opposite the piano, on a large antique sideboard with thick, ornately carved legs, Nanny's best Wedgwood china was

lovingly displayed. A big, square-shaped soup tureen, with the ladle sticking through a slit in the domed lid, sat in the centre, with the serving bowls and their matching lids displayed around it. A matching set of cheese dish, butter dish, and gravy boat with drip-dish, all clustered around on the fine, handcrafted runner, crocheted by Nanny, no doubt. A dark wooden antique carriage clock stood right in the middle of all this china. It chimed every hour on the hour; its Big Ben chimes chimed so loud that it drowned out your voice mid-sentence. George would wind it up with a key every evening and then again first thing in the morning before going to work.

Inside the sideboard there was a stack of plates and platters in the same Wedgwood pattern, largest plates on the bottom shelf, smallest on the top and a set of matching cups and saucers on the middle shelf. Elegant champagne and wine glasses, nestling in their soft blue velvet lined boxes were stacked in equal piles in the other end of the sideboard, on top of a red satin lined wooden box containing a fine bone-handled carving set and matching cutlery. All this, and much more, had its own place in the sideboard. All shipped over from Canada, no doubt, and ready for the next serving of High Tea.

In the middle of the room, stood the table with its big, fat, carved and turned legs with a complete set of leather upholstered high backed chairs. The table was covered with a green chenille tablecloth with long fringing, much like the tablecloths seen in fortune-tellers tents. A smaller, pure white cotton tablecloth was then spread over the top, to save wear and tear. A half-filled crystal decanter set, the contents written on the front, sat to the far side of the table nearest the window. Diagonally on the other side, a large cut-glass ashtray and lighter were also strategically placed, all ready for the occasional visitor. And right in the middle of the table in pride of place: a big ornate cut-glass vase was filled with an array of flowers, freshly cut from the garden. Framed portrait sized photographs of family members, softly coloured, hung around the parlour, by lengths of parcel string, from giant curly brass picture-hooks, attached to the top of the wall panelling. George's portrait stood out from the rest, looking like an airline pilot in his smart dress uniform, hat tilted slightly to one side, from his army days. I'm not sure what his post was during the war, but he had a nasty scar shaped like a stab wound in his neck. He said he got it while engaged in combat with a Ghurkha; but he was quite fond of a good story, so I'm not certain if it is true.

Most of the walls of the cottage were covered in panelling, painted in a greyish-green colour - army surplus paint no doubt. I remember running my fingers over the painted tongue-and-groove panelling of the hall and the stairs leading to the cellar. It made a nice flicking sound the faster I went. At the bottom of the stairs was the cellar, a lower ground floor leading to the garden. To the left stood a bright green old-fashioned food cabinet, with shaker-style doors with glass middles, two at the top and two at the bottom. In the middle was a display shelf. This shelf was always stacked high with newspapers and old magazines, used mainly for lighting the fire and to cover the top of the dresser to protect it from the mess of dirty forks and several half-used tins of cat-food.

Rolls of flypaper hung from the ceiling just above the dresser, to catch the flies that were drawn to the faint smell of cat-food that lingered in the warm, damp air. In the middle of the low, toffee-colour stained ceiling, with its studs of condensation poised ready to drip on your head, swung a single light bulb. It dangled from a length of knotted, brown flex, and swung gently in the breeze from the open back door. The late afternoon sun shone through the door, and the branches of the old cherry tree threw shadows across the flag stone floor like long witch's fingers trying to reach in. This gave the cellar a warm, but eerie feel.

A mountain of coal lay in the far corner of the cellar. George would constantly fill the brass coal scuttle all through the winter months, to keep ablaze the open Victorian fireplace in the back kitchen above the cellar. The sunlight pierced down into the cellar from the street above, through the many holes in the manhole cover. Large dust motes constantly rained down the golden shafts of sunlight into the semi-darkness, interrupted now and then by the shadows of people walking over it above. The floor near the wooden slatted back door, with its little iron latch, was always strewn with old bowls, filled with water and cat food. Nan loved her cats and fed many a stray. But the garden beyond was a chocolate box of delights that Gertrude Jekyll would have been proud of.

After school, Nan liked me to fetch shopping for her and George's supper from the little shop next door. She would give me a few worn black pennies for my trouble, but it was no trouble at all! Just to spend some time in her garden was more than enough payment for me. We only had a backyard at our house, but Nan had a real cottage garden and to me it was more beautiful than any manicured manor house garden.

In early Spring, after the clusters of snowdrops had withered and died, and the daffodils had faded and been carefully folded over and knotted to save their energy, bunches of tulips and blue forget-me-nots poked their way through masses of colourful wall-flowers and primroses.

The tumble-down wall partitioning the garden, brought down after the removal of an unexploded bomb during the Second World War, was now home to a multitude of tiny insects and ladybirds, hidden in a thick, lush mat of little multi-coloured daisies that wove in and out of every nook and cranny, meeting a landslide of purple aubrietia which puddled at the foot of the wall. This giant rocky landscape stained purple stood out against the white and yellow alyssum that formed their- own puddles of colour. Whilst in the dappled shade of the cherry tree, grown from a cherry stone Nan had tossed out of the window, the light breeze brought a rain of pink blossom down onto the swathes of bluebells that formed a beautiful blue carpet beneath. Hyacinths with their waxy, bell-shaped flowers clumped together, with lavender-tipped stocks and the never-ending gold and yellow of the marigold.

Every evening, around about tea-time, you could hear the birds squabbling over the ripening cherries, high in the tree. To me, this made a wonderful sight and sound. George would always spoil it though, to mine and Nan's annoyance, by waving his old football rattle around and around until they all flew away

A giant buddleia bush grew rampant in a corner of the garden, enticing the prettiest of butterflies all summer long. Sweet-smelling lily-of-the-valley, Nan's favourite perfume, ran amok. Antirrhinums in every colour grew in thick bouquets, seemingly ready to pick – we called them 'bunny-rabbits'. Heavenly scented roses, in an array of yellows and pinks through to deepest reds dropped their petals, as you brushed past. And climbers, with their variegated leaves, clambered over the ivy-covered walls, all threatening to take over and engulf the last remnants of honeysuckle, with its sweet-sickly smell, along with the purple majestic wisteria and its mini-chandeliers on their second flowering of the year. The taller plants like lupines, fox-gloves, hollyhocks and delphiniums crowded the back wall of the garden, standing to attention like passengers at Waterloo station; And in between and my personal favourites, cornflowers and flaming red poppies and other wild flowers too numerous to name, all scattering their seeds ready to boldly fill the gaps in the flowerbed, year after year.

Flowerpots stuffed with straw were balanced upside-down on sticks and placed strategically around the garden to trap the thousands of earwigs that infested the clumps of late-flowering chrysanthemums, with their giant lollypop heads, along with dahlias and asters in all different sizes and colours. Giant stalks of the now faded sunflowers towered above deep crimson fuchsias, with their contrasting ballerina-like tutu's. Later, the red berries of the holly-bush contrasting with the white berries of the mistletoe that Nan had grafted onto the cherry tree, would take over, until the first frosts of the winter set in, or snow covered everything with a thick, white blanket.

Nanny-Pots and George in Bethnal Green

Nanny-Pots lived well into her eighties. She became housebound in her old age, suffering from 'dropsy' – oedema or water-retention. After several bad falls down the winding staircases in the cottage she ended up in hospital. George and Nan were re-housed soon after because the local authorities condemned the little houses in her street and pulled them down.

She took to sitting in her wooden rocking chair, in front of the fire, in her new place, the ground floor of the low rise flat. She never left it, not seeing anyone except her family. One day George found her slumped over the pile of her beloved 'Woman's Own' magazines on the little side-table. I think she died of a broken heart from having to leave her beloved garden. It's very sad to think that the other tenants in the block never knew of her existence, even though she lived there for several years.

After her death, George took to drinking too much, and suffered from high blood pressure because of it. Several years later (and I'm sorry to say (a little to my amusement) he was found slumped dead on the toilet. The thought of it still tickles me.

George was never a 'nasty drunk'. His antics mainly had us in stitches. At one of Mum's parties he fell asleep with his finger still pressed to the doorbell. When Alan opened the door, George fell in, flat on his face, squashing the little fat cigar he had in his mouth. After he had spat out the remaining strands that were flattened against his lips, all he said was that he wasn't particularly bothered because he had been trying to finish that darned cigar since Christmas!

On another occasion, Uncle John decided that George needed walking home. But George was having none of it, declaring that it was John who needed walking home. This was such a funny sight, because they were both as drunk as skunks but still trying to hold each other up.

When I was young, after popping to the next-door shop for Nan's shopping, I trod on some folded banknotes. I bent over as though tying my shoelace, whilst I gingerly picked them up and ran indoors before anyone saw me. I don't really know how much was there, as I was too scared to unfold them. I'd never seen such large bank notes before, let alone handled any, and I was a little frightened of what to do with them. So my first instinct was to give them straight to Mum for safe keeping, with a solemn promise to treat George to some beer and Nan to some cigarettes. Later, when I mentioned my promise to Mum, she said something like not to worry about them as they had enough money of their own. She didn't mean it in a nasty way; rather that she could put the money to better use with her hungry family to feed. But every time I went around to Nan's I felt a little guilty, not because we had kept the money, but because I was never given the chance to keep my promise. It must have been ever such a lot of money, although I never begrudged Mum the money because I knew she needed it more than I did and she would make better use of it. As I predicted, that Easter was the best ever, especially for me, because there were hot-cross buns all round for supper on Good Friday, as well as a chocolate egg each on Easter morning. Dad liked us to sing the songs we had learned at school as we painted our boiled Easter breakfast eggs, in a rainbow of colours from the paint-boxes we usually received at Christmas. He sometimes sang his wartime ditties as well, blanking out the rude bits, to make us laugh.

School – and Delores!

But the best bit, that I distinctly remember, was that I was given a nice new dress, a pair of black, shiny, patent leather shoes and a pair of thick, grey tights. I felt quite grown up in my new dress as I walked to school that first day back after the Easter holidays. As in the past I always had to wear jaded frilly hand me down dresses with a cardigan and ankle socks with plimsolls. The dress was quite fitted with a zip fastener and had darts back and front to nip in the waist. It was made in a soft light grey flannelette material with a small cream lace Peter Pan collar and had three or four gold domed buttons on the chest. A slightly thicker lace ran around the hem of the puffy sleeves and it had thin cream piping that ran under the bust line and down the edges of two grey velvet ties, which emphasised my small waist when tied together at the back. I felt really quite special in my new dress returning to school. Everyone in my class took notice, even if some of the better-off girls' comments were derogatory. Like, "Where did you pinch your outfit from Swaby?" But I decided that they were just jealous, and would not let them spoil it for me.

Being one of the tallest in my class, it was decided that if I wanted to be 'in the gang', I had to prove myself first: by fighting with one of the tallest and toughest girls in the class! Delores was her name, and she came from one of the toughest large families in East London.

Delores who at 5ft.10in stood as tall as me wasn't a bully, but she sure was a tough cookie having several bullying brothers to deal with. She never seemed able to wipe her nose properly, and had a snotty candle hanging most of the time, which made her a complete outsider. One day I was goaded by my so-called friends into picking a fight with her, as they called her names. But I wouldn't do it, even if they would no longer speak to me, because in a way I felt sorry for her. Not only was she as poor as we were, I had witnessed her being verbally abused by one of her brothers, who it's said, had a bad reputation for beating up the kids in the neighbourhood. But one day after school, I did find myself fighting with Delores; I remember they pushed me into her and she retaliated by really laying into me, until I was covered in cuts and bruises.

During the school summer holidays, we were often sent to one of the other local schools for some recreation and our lunch. If it were not for our perpetual hunger and the smell of food wafting over the playground, we would not have gone because of her aggressive brothers, who were always picking fights. But having fought with Delores, the next time they decided that we needed to fight I decided to be diplomatic and speak to her about it. I said that they should all do their own dirty work, and that we should be friends. This seemed to do the trick all-round and she was regularly included in the gang after that. Besides, I don't think I could have braved another beating!

Brokesley Street and Things That Go Bump in the Night...

As far back as I can remember I have had difficulty with sleeping, because bedtime always seemed to be one big nightmare for me. From a very young age, we lived off the Mile End Road, where the trams still ran, crossing the top of our street at Brokesley Street.

We lived in the bottom half of a big, old, Victorian terraced house, made semi-detached by the presence of a bombed site beside it. The ruined houses had been demolished and some of the rubble was cleared away, but much remained. Brokesley Street was quite a sinister place for a sensitive person like me, as it was only a dozen or so houses from the older, Victorian part of Tower Hamlet's Cemetery, dark, neglected and full of shadows from the many overgrown tree and laurel bushes.

The place we played hide-and-seek most often as children was the bombed site. The Debris, as we called it, held a lot of mystery for me. The boundary wall at the back was almost as high as our houses, which were four storeys high, including a basement. This large expanse of dark brick wall ran from our garden wall, across the back of the Debris (which was as wide as three houses) and met the back wall in the garden of our neighbours the Gibson's on the other side. I think it was probably the mortuary building for the Cemetery, which would have accounted for the lack of windows and the puffs of smoke or steam that spluttered out of the long piece of pipe poking out of the top of the wall. We called this chimney 'Old Smoky' and played a version of Chicken under it. If you didn't run under the pipe immediately after it had puffed, you were called 'chicken' until you could tag someone else to do it. You had to be pretty quick, though, because if it dripped onto your head, it was still very hot! But the view from my bedroom window at night was not of this steaming old pipe, in the seemingly sinister old wall, but of the Debris. Strewn with pieces of broken glass, on a moonlit night it twinkled as though with a million stars. Even now, whenever I am driving home, looking at the distant views of night reminds me of the old Debris and its bright shining stars.

In the middle of the Debris near our garden wall stood a tall old tree, with enormous long, thick branches. We had a rope tied to one of the higher branches, with a tyre tied to the other end, to make a great swing. One day, Billy and Alan were trying to out-swing each other. Billy, the elder of the two, was a handsome lad, with blond curly hair favouring Dad's colouring and a friendly, open face. He was just as inventive and mischievous as Richmal Crompton's 'Just William'. Alan, smaller, thin and wiry, had dark straight hair, favouring Mum's complexion. They decided that if they put me into the tyre telling me to hold on tight, they could push me off the wall to get more height with the momentum of the tyre, and could then 'hitch' a swing. But they hadn't thought of the consequences that on my return I would knock them off the wall like skittles. Billy managed to dodge the swing, but poor Alan ended up blue in the face with the wind knocked clean out of him after landing on his stomach across the picket fence that sub-divided the garden. He had a long stay in hospital and then a further stay in a convalescent home. When he later developed a heart condition due to rheumatic fever, it was thought that the fall had been an exacerbating factor. He spent about a year in the convalescence home. When he returned home, all the good food, inactivity and steroids had caused him to blow up from barely seven stone to an ugly Jabber the Hutt proportion of probably thirteen stone or so! I was totally in awe of him and absolutely convinced that he was not my brother. I cried and screamed, "He's not my brother!" all night long, whilst rocking and banging my head on the wall.

His many misadventures didn't stop him from getting up to further mischief, though. I remember him telling me once of how he had knocked himself out after falling into one of the newly dug open graves whilst taking a shortcut through the cemetery on his way home in the early hours of the morning, after sneaking out of the house for a night of fun with his mates.

Opposite our house was a low-rise tenement block. We loved to run up and down the long courtyard at the back, hiding in the doorways and jumping up to slap the washing that hung in rows across the cobbled yard to the annoyance of the tenants, ringing their doorbells as we ran.

The Debris next door also served as a dumping ground for all the local residents and was strewn with mountains of rubbish, broken glass and rotting food. From the amount of chicken remains, it seemed to be the staple diet of the mainly Jewish tenants of the tenement block. Tons of stinking fly-infested chicken heads and creepy-looking claws were piled high behind the street-side Debris wall. Billy and Alan took great delight in chasing us girls around the garden with the claws, pulling on the tendons that hung out to make them move up and down, as taught to them by Dad, I remember!

Another of Dad's tricks was to thread an imaginary needle with imaginary thread, and 'pass' the needle through the tops of each of his fingers and then through his palm. By making a pulling gesture at the back of his palm and moving his fingers up and down, it made it seem as though he had sewn them together! Quite a magical trick it seemed to me!

The chicken remains and other food scraps on the Debris attracted all the local cats from around the neighbourhood, whose off-spring were a breed unto themselves! All fierce and feral, they were often born with severe diseases and abnormalities, some had tufts of hair sticking out of otherwise hairless bodies, all were covered in scabby mange, some with missing eyes, partially blind and mangled, bent-up ears. With slime hanging from their mouths and running down their matted fur and thick green mucus running from their noses due to cat flu or some other diseases, they frightened you half to death, especially if confronted by one, while playing hide-and-seek in the darkness of the old chimney recesses of the ruined buildings running up the side of our house.

This reminds me of an incident one night, when I had gone to bed, and our own domestic cat,(I don't remember its name) had got into bed with me. In came my skinny sister, Sue, with whom I shared a room. We never got on as kids, always fighting and bickering, although we're the best of friends today. As she opened the door, she asked in her usual off-hand way,
"Who the heck are you talking to?"
"The cat of course!" I snapped back.
"Can't be – I've got the cat here!"

We had a little heated debate about who had the cat and then she pulled back the curtain to let in the light from the open window. There, to my horror, was one of the ugliest, mangiest, flea-infested, drool-drenched, one-eyed specimens you would ever see in your life, and it was in my bed! I had been snuggling up to it, under the blankets, for the past hour or so.
YUCK! I still shudder to think of it!

Who's that Creeping About?

This brings me to another story, when I was old enough to know better but circumstances prevailed, and I was desperate! My sister, Diana, was the baby of the family, still in a cot in my parents' room. Diana was dark-haired with one brown and one violet eye. She is now the mother of three girls, and a complete clone of Mum, with about eight grandchildren at the last count.

I needed to go to the toilet in the middle of the night and to get to the outside toilet, you had to go down a dark stairwell and around the banisters at the bottom, passing the lounge door and along the passage, past the kitchen door and the door to the cupboard-under-the-stairs that was situated next to the heavily bolted back door. The loo was located just outside the back door in the yard. The light bulb in the loo was never working, either because it was broken, or had been taken out to be used elsewhere. You thanked God for a bright moon to light the way and shine through the cracks of the makeshift door. The wind would howl and whistle around you, blowing in from the big gap under the door and the cold night air would make you shiver.

I remember I crept out of the bedroom so as not to wake anyone. The light from the top landing was just strong enough to make out the stairs below. At the bottom of the stairs, high on the wall of the passage was a wooden coat hanger. Most of the coats that were hung there ended up on the floor, as there were too many coats and not enough hangers. As I peered into the semi-darkness I noticed, at the bottom of the stars, a small, black, shadowy shape moving about and looking as if it could be coming towards me. I dashed back into the bedroom and closed the door as quietly as I could – partly because I didn't want to wake the others, but mostly because I didn't want the 'thing' coming in after me. I stood there for what seemed like forever until I had calmed down a little and felt that my heart had stopped pounding.

I then decided to pay a visit to my parent's bedroom, which was next-door to ours, to use the dreaded tin p***-bucket, not daring to take another look down the stairs in case the spook was still there. This was a bit tricky, because the bucket was kept under my parents' bed, and was for extreme emergencies only, especially where we kids were concerned. To use it, you had to be extremely quiet. So still a little shaky from my experience, and trying hard not to wake anyone, I crept into their bedroom. But to my horror and great distress, the bucket was already full to the brim! By this time I was really desperate. So, to my utter shame and disgust, which has lasted until this very day, I decided to climb into the bottom of the cot and pee under the little one's blankets, hoping that this would go un-noticed. However, when I recently confessed this to Diana, she said she remembered this event because she had got a scolding next day for spilling her bottle of orange-juice all over the mattress!

Memories of Growing-up in Mile End

Things weren't all doom and gloom, though. On Sundays, Mum would often lie in and Dad would prepare breakfast for us - porridge oats with milk and sugar, or scrambled eggs with bread and butter.

I'd be lying in bed and the noise of the milkman's clinking bottles, as he did his round, would wake me up. The brightness of the sun, streaming through a chink in the curtains, would make me run into Mum's room and jump into her bed, snuggling up to her in the warm blankets. Sometimes I would run downstairs to the sitting room and sit with my legs over one of the arms of the big, 50's-style armchairs and just listen to the old wireless. Ed Stewpot's Two-Way Family Favourites would usually be playing, or the Overseas Broadcasting Service and sometimes The Archers.

On Sunday afternoons, the rag-and-bone man would ring his big, brass bell. This was a signal for all the women in the street to turn out their old clothes, to make extra money, and for us kids to get a free balloon. On many occasions, the clothing in his barrow was in better condition than the ones we were wearing, so Mum would barter with the rag-and-bone man to get us what we needed.

On Sunday evenings, Mum would bath all the younger ones ready for school the next day. The galvanised iron bath tub was brought into the kitchen from its hanging place outside on the garden wall. Mum would boil a big old kettle and several large pans of water on the black-leaded stove in the kitchen. The smaller ones were bathed first, two at a time to help save on hot water, then the others, one by one, as the water was topped up. So if you were last, the water would be a lot colder, and looked quite murky! If it were too cold in the kitchen, Mum would sometimes bath us in front of a roaring fire in the living room.

If the weather was hot and sunny, she would block the outside drain in the corner of the yard with old rags then fill the corner with water so we could all splash around until we were clean! The water-covered drain was coated in a film of green moss, which made it very slippery. But that made it all the more fun, as we went slipping and sliding in the warm water. All the while, above us, Mum kept a watchful eye from the open kitchen window, with her chin resting on her hands and her elbows leaning on the windowsill. I have this fond recollection of her there whenever I clean out my own garden pond! The feeling of sun-warmed water and the slimy moss under my bare feet brings back those good old memories. After she had rinsed us all off in the big tub, Dad dried and dressed us ready for bed. Dad had little time to play with us on a one-to-one basis, there was always someone needing him for odd jobs elsewhere. But these were the times when you might sometimes get a cuddle or a tickle, before bed.

Mum kept half-a-dozen chickens in a coop about halfway up the garden near the picket fence, which divided the garden into two, beneath the shade of the big tree. She fattened them up on cornmeal and worms, as well as kitchen scraps and mash. When they were fat enough, she would slaughter them by tying their legs together and chopping off their heads, something she had learned to do when she was a young girl living on the farm in Canada. One time, she forgot to tie the legs together, and when she chopped off its head, to our surprise and horror it jumped from her grasp and ran around the garden headless, with blood spurting from it everywhere and me in front of it, running and dodging as fast as I could, I could have sworn it was chasing me! Everyone thought it was very funny, except me; in fact, it gave me nightmares for a long time after.

Whilst Mum plucked and cleaned out the bird, Dad would be peeling loads of potatoes and chopping them small. He told us it was to ensure that they would be nice and crispy, but I suspect it was really to make it look as though we had far more on our plate. With a few green vegetables and a chunk of batter pudding, we would then have a nice Sunday roast dinner.

Fred and Mary

Fred and Mary Anson lived in the top two floors of our house, sharing our outside toilet and also used the fenced-off top half of the garden. They found going up and down the stairs in order to empty their rubbish into the dustbins a bit of a chore, so occasionally they wrapped their refuse in newspaper and 'lobbed' it into the Debris. Not long after one Christmas, I was playing out in the garden with my new bucket and spade, looking for worms, when a parcel fell into the garden in front of me. It fell open to reveal a huge chunk of Christmas cake, covered in very thick, white icing. I suppose it was stale, but none-the-less I took great delight in finishing it off for them.
They sometimes looked after us if Mum and Dad were running a bit late. I don't really remember myself, but Gladys told me that they used to take one or two of us upstairs to treat us to whatever they were having for tea, because they knew we would be hungry and we all looked emaciated and pale.

Fred and Mary bought a new mattress for their bed, and left the old horse-hair one on the stairs for disposal later. This was an open invitation to us to have a good time jumping and rolling down the stairs on the mattress. It was the game of the day, until I got a horse-hair splinter in the sole of my foot. Fred had to hold my foot still, whilst Mary tried to remove it with tweezers. It was quite painful because you couldn't really see it, and as they were quite elderly their eyesight wasn't as good as it was glasses were not readily available then. A lot of people wore hand-me-down glasses, from their deceased parents or relatives.

My Sister Gladys

Gladys had to wear glasses as a girl and I think that was why she was nick-named poggles glasses+ goggles= poggles somehow! She was slim and very fair, but a bit of a rebel. She often carted Sue or me over to the local churchyard 'to play' when she was really meeting up with a boy that she had made a date with. Her antics got her into serious trouble and she ended up pregnant with her first son, Andrew. She was cared for during her pregnancy by a nunnery, and had to give Andrew up for adoption, as was the norm in those days. This was all kept highly secret! She subsequently had another son, Christopher, but tragically lost him as a baby. I remember it very clearly. She had propped him up with his feed bottle and slipped out of the room for a pee or something. I looked into his cot and noticed that he was very uncomfortable, and was having trouble with his feed. But by the time Glad was alerted, it was too late and he suffocated.

It was a terrible time, with Gladys screaming and crying his name. He was a beautiful baby, with big blue eyes and thick, straight dark hair. I think this made me painfully aware of how fragile life can be at that age and gave me a deep-seated fear of having babies at too early an age. In fact, I told Mike my husband I did not want any children and only relented at twenty-five when Diana had a child at sixteen. I thought if she could cope at that age, then surely I could!

Folk Healing

In the days before the launderette, the bag-wash service went door-to-door for your washing. It came back in a big cotton bag (hence the name bag-wash) with big black numbers stamped on the side, to match your ticket. One day, whilst warming myself next to the stove, sitting on the bag-wash, I got badly scalded down one leg. Linda was making some tea and the kettle slipped from her grasp, splashing water onto me. The hot water made my leg blister from knee to ankle. Even though it was very painful, and I had difficulty walking, I quite enjoyed having that time off school, at home with Mum, getting lots of attention. Dad fixed up a swing for me in the doorway to the yard, and I would sit and swing for hours on end.

When I had to return to school Mum left the dressing off the blistered area, to let the air get to it. I think she was taught about burns dressings when she was an apprentice nurse during the war. She had pierced the blisters with a hot pin to let the fluid out, as she said it was then less likely to leave a scar. But the school nurse did not agree with this at all and every day would put a fresh dressing on it then wrap it with a big bandage. Mum would be furious and take it all back off again as soon as I got home. In the end, Mum went to the school to see the nurse, and told her that if she insisted on putting on a dressing and bandage, she (Mum) would keep me off school until all the blistering had completely healed. The nurse did as she was asked and thanks to Mum's firm action, I have no scars on my leg today.

Story-telling

On many occasions, when the electricity meter had used up its shilling, and Mum was at the shops, we would all huddle around the kitchen table in the semi-darkness. The little ones were sat in the centre, and the bigger ones sat on the edges, their feet up on the chairs. There were not enough chairs for all to sit on properly and no-one wanted to stand on the darkened floor, where we could hear all the mice scurrying around under the floorboards. Sometimes, we could hear them squeaking in the flue of the chimney breast above the old, black stove.

This was probably the time when nicknames were made up, and a good time to tell stories to keep us little ones from crying in the dark. I can remember crying with laughter on some days, or on others being frightened near witless from the spooky stories my brothers would tell. One favourite story was handed down from Dad's Dad. We called it 'Johnny I want my liver' and it went something like this:

"One day, on a shopping trip to the butchers, Johnny's Mum bought some liver for tea. That night, as Johnny was sleeping, he was awakened by a little voice calling to him, 'Johnny, I want my liver back!' He peered out from the blankets into the darkness of his bedroom and, to his horror, heard the voice again. This time it said, 'Johnny, I am outside your house, and I want my liver back!' Johnny sat bolt upright in bed hardly believing his ears. But again came the voice, this time a little louder – 'Johnny, I'm at your street door and I want my liver.

Johnny dived back down into bed and pulled the covers over his head. But again he heard the voice calling to him – 'Johnny, I'm on the first stair and I want my liver" and then again 'Johnny I'm on the second stair and I want my liver"

One stair after another, the story-teller repeats the voice, all the way to the top stair, gradually getting louder and louder. Without pausing, the voice appears to be outside Johnny's door, inside Johnny's room, next to Johnny's bed, until finally the storyteller grabs the person next to them, yelling, "GOTCHA!" Don't try telling this story to those of a nervous disposition, in the dark!

I don't know a lot about Dad's family. I know he was fostered at a young age, and later as a young man of barely 18, he joined the army. He was mainly based around the Essex area. It was all the spud-bashing on kitchen duties that perfected his skill at peeling potatoes!

When he was quite ill, I used to take him home to Harold Hill, to spend the weekend or so with me. We would drive to the local stream at Navestock Side, for a picnic and to get some fresh air. We would sit and paddle our feet in the stream and relax as we ate our picnic. He thought the area looked familiar, as he had been based quite near there, possibly at Hornchurch although he could not remember exactly where. This was quite a nice time for me, reminiscing about the old days and getting to know him a little better. We remembered the time he fell down the cellar stairs. At the foot of the stairs, two large hooks protruded from one of the cellar beams. These hooked into his trouser legs and suspended him, upside down, for several minutes. Winded, with all the breath knocked out of him, he was unable to speak. I screamed blue murder for someone to come and help me unhook him, with tears streaming down my face, as I was sure he must be dead! We laugh at it now, though – it was like something out of an old Laurel and Hardy film.

As a family, there was quite a lot of humour. Linda and Gladys shared their beds with Susan and me, in the back room at Brokesley Street, (2 up 2 down). One morning, Sue and I were trying very hard to stifle our giggles. We were under strict instructions that on no account were we to wake either of them up first thing in the morning, because there would be hell to pay, especially on a Sunday morning when they liked to lie-in. We watched in gleeful anticipation as a great big spider, on a single thread of web, floated down from the ceiling, heading straight for Linda's open mouth as she snored, blissfully unaware! We tried in vain to stifle our giggles, with both hands stuffed into our mouths, while sitting at the end of the bed. Luckily for us (and for her) she woke up just in time to see it. But there was still hell to pay for having NOT woken her up to tell her. You just couldn't win!

Then there were the times we used to bring big old cardboard boxes home from the factory at the top of the street, to play in. They were very unusual in shape, they looked like cardboard coffins. I'm still not sure what they were used for!

And the times I used to race Alan down the street on our skates. It must have looked quite daft, because we literally shared a pair of skates - one each!

Then there was the time Bill made a kind of ghost house down in the cellar of Coborn Road. He frightened the living daylights out of his best friend, Dennis Evans, by betting him that he would not go down the stairs in the dark to put a shilling in the meter at the back of the cellar. Whilst he was down there fumbling with the money trying to find the meter slot, Bill crept down behind him to give him the fright of his life. In the darkness the ceiling was hung low with cobwebs shredded from old net curtain so as to touch your face as you walked by. The guy we used for Guy Fawkes night to collect pennies was given a new lease of life, so to speak, it was placed in the middle of the room with a white skeletal face tucked under a long haired grey wig and sat in an upright position in a cardboard shaped coffin, ready and waiting to be illuminated with a red light as the shilling dropped into the electric box. You never saw anyone run up a flight of stairs so quickly. I'm sure he had several grey hairs the next day!

Another ingenious idea of Bill's was his attempts to entertain us with amusing stories that he recorded on an old tape deck. But he would replace the voices with dialogue pre-recorded from funny programs on TV and radio. The effect had us rolling around with laughter and with tears in our eyes. I think Monty Python did a similar sketch called 'The Ministry of Funny Walks', and sketches of the Queen and her family and other VIPs with voice-overs. I think Bill must have got there first as I don't remember seeing the Monty Python show until much later, after I was married.

Coborn Road – More Things That Go Bump…

I was glad when we eventually moved from Brokesley Street to Coborn Road. Dad managed to borrow an old market barrow and move us bit by bit to Coborn Road, on the other side of the Mile End Road. I managed to break my nose during the move. I had perched myself on the mantelpiece and I fell off onto the iron frame of the bedstead Dad was unscrewing at the time. It was a much bigger house, with an upstairs bathroom and toilet, and another indoor toilet just off the kitchen. It had two living rooms, a dining room and a large cellar, plus a small garden. And we didn't have to share it with another family.

But my glee was short-lived because Coborn Road had its own ghost, an old man who had lived there before, he was murdered. The house had been converted from the man's large jewellery and work-shop. It was said that he regularly shut up shop for lunch at two o'clock. Mum swore that she regularly heard him shutting the door when she was there on her own. It didn't matter how carefully you kept an eye out for him, you never saw anything. But the minute your back was turned, you heard the door slam shut at about the same time every day. Billy said he thought he saw his ghost in the little back bedroom which he used as a jewellery workshop. It was there that he apprehended a burglar and was bludgeoned to death. Billy had just gone to bed that night in the back room, when he heard a rattle as though a window was being opened or closed. Peering out from the covers he felt a cool breeze on his face and saw the dark, shadowy shape of a short, stout man just leaving the room. I could swear that I had felt a presence there, too, whilst sleeping in the room with Sue when Dad redecorated our own bedroom.

Bill was working away from home at the time, in a large hotel in Northumberland. As a young teenager, I missed my big chance of working away from home with him. Mum told me that he had come home unexpectedly one night, on a flying visit, with the intention of taking me back with him to be trained as a chambermaid. But I had gone out for the day to the seaside with a friend and her family and by the time I returned home, to my complete and utter disappointment, he had already left on his return journey

I think, because of its murky past, Sue and I were glad to get out of that room and back into our own, although it was probably only a little better. The light bulb would constantly flicker, or just burn out, and to find another one to replace it was something short of a miracle. Sometimes, you had to use your wits, and surreptitiously swap your dead bulb for someone else's working one – usually the one in the boys' bedroom. However, nine times out of ten, they would cotton on and pinch it back again. So we often had to rely on the light from the bulb in the hall and landing outside. You just wouldn't dare to swipe that one, because it would mean having to come up the stairs in the dark. It gives me the creeps thinking about it. Also, on a number of occasions, I felt that I was being pushed up against the wall, and all the breath was being squeezed out of my body, making it impossible to scream. But by what, I do not know. So even though I had had a couple of weird experiences in our bedroom, I never felt threatened like I did in those downstairs rooms, so it was a relief to get back to normal, if you could call it that.

Another time I brought back a wooden orange box from the market. It was made of plywood, with a hinged lid and the country of origin stamped in orange and green on the sides. You'd see them discarded in huge piles on the pavement on market day. I thought it would be a great idea to rub it down and paint it, to make a nice bedside cabinet. But Mum saw me bringing it in and told me in a no uncertain manner to get it out of the house immediately. So like all children, I snuck it in and covered it with an old tablecloth. I don't know if it was an overactive mind combined with a guilty conscience, but that night, to my horror, the whole thing seemed to rise up and fly about in the air. I looked on terrified from my bed, and needless to say I flung it out first thing in the morning before anyone else got up.

Some years later, the boys decided that they would like to swap bedrooms with me and Sue. So we moved into the larger room with the en-suite bathroom at the end, that night. But my night-time terrors were not confined to the back bedroom – there were a few unnatural things going on in this room, too! Like no matter how many times, or how firmly, you shut the bathroom door at night, it would always be wide open in the morning. And no matter how often, or how tightly, you turned the bath-taps off, come morning they would be drizzling away. I suppose there is a logical answer there somewhere, but as there was no other access to the bathroom apart from through our bedroom, it still remains a mystery to us all.

One time I thought I heard the sound of a newspaper being read. I distinctly heard the pages being turned over slowly, one by one. But it was too dark to see anything and the noise seemed to be coming from under my bed, so I just pulled the pillow over my head to block off the sound and tried to dismiss it as just my imagination!

Another time, I woke to see someone out of the corner of my eye, walking past the end of my bed and disappearing near Sue's bed at the far end of the bedroom, like someone had just turned off the light and got into bed. I'd not heard anyone come into the room, so assumed it must have been Sue. I called her name but she did not answer, so I looked towards her bed, and in the darkness I could just make out her shape, moving about under the covers. Again, a little louder, I called Sue, but still she did not reply, but I thought I heard a deep sigh. As she is a little deaf, I called out quite loudly, almost shouting her name. With that, the bedroom door flew open and Sue's head popped round the door as she yelled back, "Yeah! What do you want?" I mumbled something like I thought it was her, but I didn't dare tell her of my experience as I didn't think she would ever sleep in her bed again and I didn't want to sleep in that room alone that night, or any other night, for that matter!

I had no choice really, as the rest of that big old house was just as spooky. If you slept downstairs, the trek to the loo, which was located just off the kitchen at the back of the house, was a bit of a nightmare. First you had to walk the length of a dark hall, past the cellar door, then through the back living room with the smouldering cinders in the fire-grate throwing shadows all around the now cold room, with its grubby three-piece suite and threadbare carpet. You daren't turn on the light because more often than not Uncle John would be sleeping it off on the sofa. Then you carried on through a small dining room with its creaking floorboards and huge old open fireplace that spilled cockroaches all over the floor (which I once had the misfortune to tread on one night!). Mum had a big old Smeg refrigerator in there, with a tall old-fashioned food cupboard opposite it. What was supposed to be the dining table was always stacked with washing in piles of dirty, clean, awaiting putting away etc. Because it was next to the small narrow kitchen, Mum also kept her twin-tub washing machine in there too. This was her pride and joy – quite a luxury for her in those times. I sometimes thought that the only things the house had going for it was that it had an inside toilet and a room where Mum could have her own washing machine. We did have a big old-fashioned television set in the sitting room – but Dad had removed the on/off switch at some time, so that we kids did not waste electricity turning it on at all hours when he and Mum were not there. We learned to turn it on using a pair of pliers and it was quite funny one evening when a friend of Sue's asked what the pliers were doing on the TV set, to be told that they were there to turn the TV on of course! What else! This was quite normal for us.

On another frightening occasion, I felt something jump onto the end of my bed. I was so frightened that I had to convince myself that it was just the cat, or even fairies, before I would even contemplate a peep from below the covers. After what seemed an eternity, I gingerly pulled the blankets down from over my head and there to my utter horror, in the light of the full moon, crouching at the end of my bed, was something that looked like all my worst nightmares rolled into one! I can only describe it as a little goblin-type creature, with a big, fat, bald head. Its head was almost as big as its naked, hairless body. It had large, pixie-like ears, a long nose, and large, round, menacing eyeballs. His crooked teeth were sharpened into points, in a slimy, wet mouth, and he was grinning at me, from ear to ear. Quick as a flash, I pulled the bedclothes back up over my head whilst at the same time letting out the biggest scream that I could muster! This woke Mum, who came running to see what was happening, but by that time it had disappeared. To calm me down, Mum said she would leave the landing light on for a while, until she thought I had dropped off to sleep. But I still had to sleep in that room, sometimes on my own, so I got into the habit of going to bed early in the hope of dropping off before it got dark!

This was not the last I saw of that creature, though. Once, on a sleepover at a friend's house we were mucking about with the Ouija board. That evening, when the three of us went to bed, there was a huge shadow on the bedroom wall, in the shape of that goblin. We could all see him, and when we looked out of the window, there he was sitting in a tree! Later on, I promised my sister, Lin, that we would not use the Ouija board again, as she said you can conjure up all sorts of evil spirits with it if you do not use it properly.

I recently asked one of the said friends to confirm that this really happen and she said that it was a little hazy but she did remember it.

My Sister Linda

I used to baby-sit for Lin and her husband, Leslie. I thought it was great – anything to get away from that spooky old house, and stay in her nice, warm, modern flat with its shiny, tiled floors.

She used to play a game of 'polish the floor' with her baby son, Anthony. He would be seated on the top of a big, polishing mop and towed up and down. He thought it was great fun, laughing and giggling all the while, as the waxed floors were buffed to a good shine. She let me 'ride' the mop as well, but because I was a good deal bigger and taller, I always fell off – but it was great fun!

As a young woman, before she met and married Les, she would practise rock and roll and her jive technique with a high-backed chair as a partner. She went to lots of West End clubs and met several up and coming stars, including Cliff Richard (who was plain old Harry Webb then) and enjoyed a couple of dates with him. She's been happily married to Les now for a number of years. Les was a clever boy with a chemistry/science interest, who went on to become Managing Director of a manufacturing company. They have two children, several grandchildren, and live in a beautiful thatched cottage in the middle of the countryside now. Having to return to that big old house after staying at Lin's neat little flat all weekend was a nightmare.

Christmas Revels

Christmas was one of the big special occasions in our house and something to look forward to. Every Friday Dad would go up to the Coburn Arms pub, on the corner of the street, to pay some money from his pay packet into the Christmas Savings Club. The money saved ensured a good Christmas and was used to buy our presents and beer and spirits for the New Year's Eve party. Mum would also order the biggest hamper from the Hamper Club. In the days before we moved to Coborn Road, Co-op cheques paid for these, as well as new clothes, school uniform and shoes. Then Mum and Dad worked hard all year to pay back the debt. Later, the Government introduced a scheme to give vouchers for needy families like ours.

The big front room at Coborn Road was usually kept locked, and only opened for Christmas, weddings, christenings, New Year's Eve and other party occasions. It was sometimes opened to allow us to do our courting in there if we were 'serious', and very occasionally as a spare bedroom, if Dad was decorating. But it was also a very spooky room as it was the old shop front with a partition to hide the workshop behind it which we used as a bedroom and I hated having to sleep in there.

At Christmas, the whole room would be given a good spring-clean, which we all loved giving Mum a hand with. A fire was laid in the newly polished grate and kept ablaze throughout. As the preparations were put into place, there was a buzz of excitement going all around the house throughout the day. Mum always put on an amazing show of decorations, with help from us kids. We always had the biggest tree down the street, with ornaments kept in the cupboard from year to year. There was a selection of gold and silver glass baubles that hung from every branch. Large fancy fairy lights gave a warm glow to the room whilst bouncing little stars of light off the strands of tinsel that constantly twirled in downward spirals as we busied ourselves around the room. Chocolate snowmen, Father Christmases and little bags of chocolate money, were also hung on the branches, as were brightly painted rocking horses and drummer boys carved from wood.. On New Year's Eve we took great delight in our share of these chocolate treats, if there were any left! We thought of it as our reward for the hard effort of preparing the room. On the top of the tree, Mum placed a big fairy doll, dominating the tree with its big, glittering, feathery wings and layers of crinoline lace petticoats, edged with ruffles of silver and gold tinsel. Then, before bed, we would hang our stockings, actual socks, on a line slung across the mantelpiece and in turn shout up the chimney to Father Christmas, to tell him what we wanted.

Late on Christmas Eve, the smouldering red embers of the dying fire in the darkened grate were just light enough for you to make out the long line of stockings, full of hopeful wishes. This was the most magical sight, for anyone who had the courage to creep downstairs and peep into the room in the wee small hours to see if Father Christmas had been to our house yet on that very special night of Christmas Eve.

Mum would have decorated an old tea chest with white crepe paper, and tied a red crepe-paper ribbon with a huge red bow, around it. Into the chest went the presents that she had been buying over the last few weeks, all lovingly wrapped and labelled. There were always at least three presents each, and you always got at least one thing you had asked Father Christmas for on Christmas Eve. The stockings had been magically transported to the bottoms of our beds and they were filled to bursting with all sorts of nice things. Always an apple in the heel and an orange in the toe, and in-between chocolate money, shelled nuts, shiny new pennies, and sometimes small presents.

After breakfast, we would all gather together in front of the blazing fire in the front room, all sat on the floor looking forward with eager anticipation to receiving our presents. It was a tradition and an honour, to be 'Father Christmas' that year, and give out the gifts that Mum and Dad fished out of the tea chest. Christmas dinner was a lavish affair for us. We all sat at an enormous long table made from two ordinary tables with an old door bridging the gap in the middle. It was covered with several white cotton sheets, and Mum's best tablecloths. A holly-berry wreath, tied up in loops of red ribbon and with a candle in the middle acted as the centrepiece, and crackers were set with the knives, forks and spoons to mark each place. Chairs were brought from all over the house, with several benches improvised from boards set across two chairs to provide additional seating. Dad sat at the head of the table, and would carve the turkey, whilst Mum served the roast potatoes and Yorkshire puddings. We helped ourselves to the array of traditional vegetables. After dinner, we would fill the corners with a slice of Mum's homemade Christmas pudding, served with custard or cream. If you were really lucky, you might find a new sixpence in your slice of pudding. After dinner, we usually played with our new toys and games, or watched the Christmas Special film on TV.

All the family were invited round for tea and the house would be at bursting point. Auntie Nance, Mum's younger sister from South Ockendon, with her husband Ernie and their brood of daughters, Kathy, Jenny, Elaine, Mandy, and jacpuline. Uncle John, Nan, and Mum's younger brother George would be there, and most of our neighbours would come along especially to see Mum's decorations. Uncle George would often 'fall asleep' on the sofa, and me and Sue would have great fun putting his hair in rollers and slapping on outrageous make-up. Aunties and Uncles we may not have seen all year would drop in, too. One particular uncle, Bill, had a motor-bike and he would give Gladys, who was in her early teens at the time, rides around the streets where we lived, much to the disapproval of his wife, Joyce my Godmother. Joyce's father, Bill Turner, would also come along. He rode in the motorcycle's sidecar. After first removing his wooden legs, he would hoist himself in, then Joyce would sit in the space where his legs would have been, and Aunt Rose rode pillion behind Bill.

In the evening, we would all play a family game, such as 'Bingo!' Dad would call the numbers and Mum would help us younger ones to fill in our bingo-card. Later, we would move on to simple card games, which invariably led up to adults-only card games that went on late into the evening, after our bed times, or until Aunt Nance and Uncle Ernie (who were never called by their real names of Shirley and Eddie, goodness knows why), had to make a start for their long journey home.

The first Boxing Day after their marriage, Lin and Les came home for tea. Les's obviously good up-bringing must have unnerved Mum, because Les was surprised to be served up a hot steak-and-kidney pie with custard for his 'afters'! Mum had had to dig deep into the freezer to get what she thought was an apple pie, and they must have looked much the same in their frozen state. Les was too well mannered to say anything until Lin, seeing him pushing it around his plate, asked what was wrong. He whispered that the apple pie tasted funny, and was full of brown stuff, like gravy! Lin told Mum of her mistake and Mum, even more flustered, brought Les another plate of apple-pie and custard. To Les's dismay and consternation, that one, too, was steak-and-kidney. He took it all in good part and he and Mum joked about it for years after. Mum was ribbed by the rest of us for years, too!

Another funny time was when Dennis, Bill's friend, was waiting for Bill to get ready to go out for a night on the town. Seeing the baby, Janet, in the cot with some sweeties, he asked her for one. As he picked her up from the cot for a cuddle to make her laugh, to his surprise, she popped one of the Maltesers into his laughing mouth. He took a bite, and discovered, to his horror, that it was in fact the contents of her nappy! Putting the baby down very quickly, he ran into the kitchen yelling for hot water and washing-up-liquid, before sticking his head under the tap in an attempt to wash out his mouth. Deciding that even that was not enough, he ran home, froth spilling from his mouth, to try to clean his teeth with toothpaste. I don't think they had any luck with the girls that night, either!

Mum's Sister, Nance

As a special treat in the summer, Mum would sometimes take us out for the day to visit Aunt Nance and her girls, our cousins, at their house in South Ockendon. We all thought they were so lucky, living in the countryside with beautiful views of the rolling hills and going to the stables to ride whenever they liked.

It took the best part of the day to get there by travelling on the Green Rover bus, and I was always travelsick. But as soon as we got there, all the discomfort was forgotten because we had such fun. Aunt Nance had a pretty garden, where she used to grow her own fruit and vegetables. She had several mature fruit trees that always seemed to be laden with fruit and she would get us girls to pick them to take home for Mum to make fruit pies with. Aunt Nance would always lay on a nice spread for us, and sometimes we would eat it as a picnic on the green, after a game of Rounder's – Swaby family versus Newell family, Mums included!

Phoenix School

Our first years at school were probably some of the best for Sue and me, because we attended Phoenix Open-Air mixed School. Intended for sick and deaf children,(it was 'open-air' in that weather permitting), most of the lessons were taken outside and where you had to walk from the hall along an open-walled corridor, with a steel structured canopy roof, which crossed the perimeter of the playground to get to the classrooms on the other side. We walked these corridors come rain or shine most of the year, although in the very depths of winter they would close the glass doors. Many of the lessons were held outdoors in the extensive gardens. Story-time was held under the weeping willow tree on a grassy bank outside our classroom windows.

I have vivid memories of my first ever kiss, under the weeping willow tree, at story-time. He said he thought I wanted a kiss, as I listened intently with elbows resting on my knees, holding my chin in my hands and lips pouting. The trouble was he had a bad case of eczema from head to toe! I scrubbed my face raw when I got homes and had nightmares for a week, thinking I was going to catch it. Thinking back, Phoenix was probably the best school I ever attended because, besides a rudimentary education, we were well cared for and well fed, with breakfast, lunch and tea provided and milk and biscuits in between at playtimes. Breakfasts always consisted of scrambled egg with a slice of buttered bread on the side. The eggs were very nice, but the bread less so, as it absorbed the liquid from the egg and went soggy, which made me feel sick. The thought of it even today still makes me cringe. Lunch was a proper meal of meat, potatoes and vegetables, with pudding and custard to follow. We always got second helpings because we were always hungry and a bit on the skinny side, so the dinner ladies probably thought we needed it. The truth was that we never got enough to eat at home, because of lack of money; although our parents tried their best, there were a lot of mouths to feed. Midday playtime was followed by a rest period, where from the most senior pupil down to the youngest junior, would lie down on little folding camp beds for an hour rest. Then after our afternoon lessons followed by playtime, we were treated to a nice hot mug of cocoa or Ovaltine with a slice of bread and jam for tea.

One boy at the school sticks in my mind in particular. He always walked around with his hand in his pocket at playtime, even while playing football or table tennis. We were told that he had had a whitlow on his finger that had turned septic and he had to have his finger amputated. Sometime later, his hand was amputated, then his arm until eventually he no longer came to school and we were told that he had died. This rather alarming story saddened us all because, as one of the senior boys, he was well liked.

One day, Sue and I were fighting over the ownership of a navy blue cardigan. Sue insisted that it was hers, but I knew it was mine because hers had a hole in the elbow, and as mine didn't – that was why Sue wanted it. I was the taller of the two of us and the teacher, thinking I was also the oldest and suspecting that the cardigan was in fact mine, decreed that it should go to the oldest child. She was as surprised as the rest of the school when Sue said that SHE was the eldest, by a year and a day. After the catfight, it was decided to put us in separate classrooms. Sue said how much she hated being separated, but I thought it served her right for pinching my cardigan!

PART TWO

Marriage to Michael Coade

In the early Seventies, just before Mum and Dad moved to the Grove Road maisonette, I met Michael Coade through his younger brother, when borrowing some of his records. Michael lived in Trellis Street, just around the corner from where we lived. One day, after chatting to him on his doorstep for half-an-hour or so, his Mum invited me in, thinking I was his girlfriend – and the rest is history. Michael wore his thick, dark, curly hair to his shoulders, and had a cheeky grin. He worked as a postman at the local sorting office, and wore a dated old postman's uniform. But at weekends his appearance was transformed and he cut quite a dash in the latest made-to-measure tonic suits with red braces – the trademark of the 'Mods' – over a Ben Sherman shirt and black leather brogues. Two years later on the twenty second of April 1972 the day of our wedding at Poplar Civic Registry Office in Bow, east London, Mike's friends and colleagues at the post office formed a nice archway of the instruments from the Post Office Union Band for us to walk under.

I wore a two-piece navy blue suit, edged with yellow piping around the short sleeves of the jacket and the hem of the mini skirt over a white blouse with a pointed collar, which was extremely fashionable then. I had yellow leather 'national' shoes, like the style worn by flappers, and white tights. My Mary Quant hairstyle was topped off with a matching beanie hat with a flower over the brim. We both wore a double-red- carnation corsage, and I was presented with a couple of horseshoes and a rolling pin for luck as was the custom then.

Mike wore a brown velvet jacket over a white shirt with a brown and beige tie. His matching brown trousers had a beige panel running down the back to knee-length and he wore one-and-a-half inch black Cuban heeled shoes. I think the only time he ever came within an inch of being as tall as me was when he wore his Cuban heels, but alas, they soon went out of fashion.

Mike also comes from a large family, with six brothers and three sisters. Esther, his mother, was a strong Irish woman, with a strong Irish accent, whom I came to love dearly. She had been left to bring up her large family when their father died in his early forties. Never the less, she always looked smart and the house was as neat and tidy as she was. Her kind and loving nature and her words of wisdom with a cuddle for everyone that brought a smile to your face, are dearly missed. I thought she was a wonderful mother and endeavoured to follow in her footsteps.

After our registry office wedding, a feast of Wimpy and chips was the order of the day, washed down with a couple of whisky-and-cokes in the local pub. Our best man Philip de Baptist had the cheek to ask if he could sleep over for the night in our small flat with his new girlfriend, Linda, who accompanied him to our wedding as a witness.

As a bit of a joke, on a Post Office Beano to the seaside, not long after our wedding, I stuffed a cushion up under my dress, which got quite a reaction, especially from the older guys on the coach. But there was even more of a reaction when we returned to the coach without it!

We wasted no time moving into our first little flat on the fourth floor of Pelham Buildings in Deal Street. We had two bedrooms, a small living room with an electric fire and a tiny kitchenette. There was no bathroom and no outside space except for the view of the courtyard below our living room window that got increasingly noisy as day turned to night, especially at the weekend at turning out time at the local pub, when the men folk wandered home the worse for wear; then all hell broke loose with arguments echoing all around the courtyard, sometimes lasting late into the early hours of the following morning. But as lonely as I felt on my own at times, love knows no bounds and we loved it there all the same; in fact, we sometimes recorded the arguments and played them back at full volume out of the living room window at night, whilst having a good laugh at all the swearing going on.

This area in East London was one of Jack the Ripper's haunts and the area hadn't improved much since those Victorian days. A few street lights placed periodically along the long road highlighted the old dilapidated houses, each with the yawning darkness of the cellar areas beneath their rag-draped, grimy front windows. The cellar areas, each protected by iron gratings, lined up in rows along the pavement. These areas were alive with giant rats, and the occasional feral cat with her brood of diseased and malformed kittens crying and screeching into the night. I was petrified coming home after dark and intimidated by having to walk past drunks, or the homeless, sleeping in doorways or the graveyard, their bundles and dirty bedding spilling onto the pavement.

Three years later, along with our daughter Zoë, I was delighted to be offered a modern townhouse in Arbour Square on the other side of Valance Road in Stepney Green. Lin and Les both loved the house and thought it had bags of character, and a lovely location in a bright, leafy square. They thought we should try to buy it, but I was never happy with its layout. So we were again rehoused, this time out of town to another townhouse in Harold Hill, Essex

Harold Hill

We settled there for the next twenty-eight years to a fuller and richer life. The children kept their first pony at the local stables, a little grey called Smokey and learning to ride became a priority. Even when Michael lost some of his initial enthusiasm, Zoë and I became more involved and in her adolescent years we had two horses together called Sasha and Cochise. We spent many happy hours riding over the beautiful countryside of Havering-Atte-Bower.

But it wasn't all plain sailing; I was quite a strict mother and liked things done methodically, so a clean and tidy house was a must. I got the children used to tidying their toys and stuff away before I set out their clothes in the evening, then after their bath around nine we'd tuck them up with a story at bedtime. Then in the morning, I would make sure they hadn't forgotten anything, before seeing them across the main road to the local junior school; after which I would set about doing the household chores. In senior school they also helped lay the breakfast table the nights before school; and I left strict instruction they were not to wake me until they had eaten and had washed and brushed their teeth, before getting dressed ready to go.

Mike was a bit of a stickler for time keeping, his dinner had to be served at the same time every day, and if I said I would only be half an hour chatting to the neighbours, he'd be on at me if I was a minute or two late. Even time spent mucking out at the stables was made uncomfortably tight at times, until Zoë was old enough to be left at the yard on her own. Even if I was late getting home from my job as assistant manageress at our local charity shop, he'd phone me there to see what was keeping me, or he'd turn up outside to hurry me up (much to the annoyance of my manageress). This led to untold bickering and argument between us. That said he has a lot of good qualities, like the fact that we never got into any real debt, apart from the one encumbrance sustained while living at Pelham building. The interest rate of the HP repayment on our first ever new bedroom suite was so extortionate, he promised never to pay by instalment ever again.

He worked hard for little pay as a postman, so after work he drove around the street of London equipped with a map and a board attached to his moped. With his astute mind just twenty seven months or so later he passed 'The Knowledge' to become a fully-fledged black taxi driver, thus gaining lots of free time throughout the week that we mainly spent with the children. We had great fun teaching them how to cycle and roller-skate; and they loved to swim at the local baths, each gaining bronze, silver and gold certificates at school. And on long walks in the local forest and country parks, we taught them about the flora and fauna while having fun playing hide and seek. Sometimes we'd go for a picnic on the beach with his mum and siblings and we'd muck about for hours in a rubber dingy or snorkel in the sea. And if we got the chance on Bank Holiday weekends we'd go caravanning and take their friends along at times. Where after a full day's excursions, we'd spend the evenings having fun in the club house, or we'd just chill playing board games around the BBQ. And for two weeks in July at our Mediterranean beachside timeshare, Mike would spend hours in the pool playing rough and tumble, teaching them how to dive off his shoulders, while perfecting their underwater skills. We also enjoyed an extensive itinerary of sightseeing tours and entertainment programs that invariably led to the final ritual of the fancy dress party at the end of our stay. In the winter months we regularly spent three weeks in a Spanish hotel in the Costa-Brava, enjoying much of the same.

Some of our more exotic holidays include a month in Orlando Florida. We stayed in a Davis Brothers motel on International Drive and made full use of its curb side pool after long hot day trips out. We also braved a helicopter trip over Universal Studios, and on another trip we took an airboat hovercraft across the crocodile infested Everglade's National Park. There we visited a crocodile farm and an Indian reservation, where we saw how they lived a simple life in a Tepee and how they made a living from the sale of hand crafted jewellery and hand stitched moccasins cut from locally sourced buckskin hide. We also saw the killer whale, Shamu, perform some wonderfully amazing tricks at SeaWorld. And at the MGM studios which featured 'Indiana Jones' in a spectacular shootout around a collapsed temple of doom, we took a ride through an unnerving explosion of fire from a makeshift mineshaft, closely followed by a ferocious burst of cold water cascading down from an exploding water tower, as we gaily passed under the overhang of smouldering stilts that had once been attached to its rusty twisted metal remains. Plus we spent another four days in Disneyworld with its amazing rides and Disney characters, featuring 'Tinkerbelle' flying over the Magic Kingdom. And as night fell, from our view on the hill we watched the grand finale, a backdrop of breathtakingly beautiful fireworks lighting up the whole grand scenario. And lastly at the theme park set in the heart of Disneyworld we learned a great deal at Epcot (an acronym for Experimental Prototype Community of Tomorrow resort) which had two distinct pavilions, future world features technological innovations and world showcase (where your spoilt for choice) shares with its guests the culture and cuisine of its eleven countries.

On another memorable three-week trip we toured the Golf Coast of Florida Keys, where much to our delight in a wonderful place called Sunset Cove we got the chance to feed and swim with Manatee (sea cow). And in the world renowned Ron Johns on Coco Beach, we bought the kids a surfboard each and played at surfing. In Tampa Bay we took the sky train over the dinosaur-infested terrain of Bush Gardens. We also stayed in a high-rise beach front apartment in Clearwater that had stunning sea views and great beach bar entertainment. We visited a lot of different places while there, but these stick in my mind as being some of the best and most enjoyable!

Living in London for the first part of our married life, we had a great social life, which centred around a Walthamstow football social club, where Mike played centre-forward and centre-half. But after a badly broken leg, he reluctantly gave it all up, which left us with no social life outside of family and close friends. One day searching through the local newspapers for information, I came across a Scuba Diving Club just a short distance from our new home in Harold Hill. At just forty-two years old, I wasn't quite ready to settle for the 'TV and carpet-slippers' and quite liked the idea of an adventure. After much debate with Mike, who liked the relaxation bit after working hard, I decided to hang the expense and give it a go, albeit on my own. However, I secretly hoped that Mike would come around to it and give it a go. I helped his thinking along a bit by cajoling and bribery by offering to pay for the course for him for his fortieth birthday. It made good sense to me, as we had all loved snorkelling in our family holidays abroad.

Michael and Zoë

I share another favourite hobby, playing the guitar, with my son, Michael, the younger of my two children, of whom I'm very proud. Michael spent a year back-packing across Australia on his own, then a further six months travelling half-way across the world. Starting in Korea, he visited Japan, New Zealand, Hong Kong, China, Mongolia and Russia. He made his way back on the Trans-Siberian railway where he met up with Zoë (who is also well travelled) in Germany with her Dutch husband-to-be, Jort. The three of them then made their way back by car via the scenic splendour of Switzerland to Italy, Rome, to the place where Zoë and Jort first met and were to be wed on the 5th September, 2008. After the marriage ceremony at the beautiful Roman Chapel off the Via de Valle Delle Camene, we had a photo shoot tour in an air condition coach around the sights of Rome follow by a lavish Italian-style Wedding Feast.

Zoë and Jort now live in Holland, where she had her horse Mia, shipped over when she first went to live there in 2004. Zoë, of whom I'm equally proud, gained the necessary qualifications to become a Parelli Natural Horsemanship Instructor which also involves a lot of travelling around the world with return trips to the USA once in a while to top up her education.

End Note

After years of over-sensitivity to whatever came my way, I have now decided that it doesn't matter in the least what kind of house you have lived in, be it old spooky ones like my childhood homes, or nice new ones with all mod cons, like the ones my children were brought up in. If you are sensitive you will imagine all sorts of things, real or not, wherever you are. As has been demonstrated to me and Mike over the past years by our daughter, Zoë – but that's another story!

PART THREE

Scuba Diving - Trainee Diver

Over the last twenty years, Mike and I have shared the wonderful world of scuba diving. This hobby has taken us all over the country and to the other side of the world. We have met a diverse selection of people, from all walks of life, but bound by the pleasure of scuba diving. We have a sense of the close camaraderie that comes from belonging to a Club devoted to our main pastime, spending a lot of our time with people sharing the same interest.

This deep interest did cause me some concern when Mum was tested positive for liver cancer whilst we were halfway through our training. But she took a great interest in what we were doing and encouraged me to complete the course. I found that the intense concentration helped me to forget, if only for a few hours, the reality of her cancer

I was not an easy person to train. I'm not the brightest of sparks when it comes to the theory side of things. Amongst other things, I had great difficulty in just clearing my mask under water, even in our local swimming pool that was only three metres at its deepest. So I was passed from one training officer to another over a period of about three months. But I gave it my best shot, knuckling down and studying hard for the theory aspect, and putting lots of extra practice at the pool. Eventually, I was rewarded for my efforts with an eighty-four percent pass, and nominated for the Novice Diver of the Year Award for my perseverance.

At the annual dinner-dance the following Christmas, I was the proud recipient of the Novice Diver of the Year Winner's Plaque, with my name and the date, 1993, engraved on it. I had never won an award before, apart from a book at school for good attendance! So I'd like to say I'm extremely grateful to all those people involved in my training, those who voted for me and thanks Mum for keeping me going.

You're not just dumped into the sea after your pool training with BSAC (the British Sub Aqua Club). You have to go on and perfect your techniques in 'Save and Rescue' and learn compass work in the sea. Initially, your skills are assessed in the local lakes, Crystal Waters in my case. A complete misnomer – there is nothing 'crystal' about those waters. The quarry at Gildenburgh is a lot clearer, but it is a lot further away. A couple of the instructors, Ted and Christine Bonner, regularly helped out with our training, and after the training session we would often clock up some dive time, in readiness for our deep-sea diving. On one such training dive, I lost one of my fins in the mud. Ted had warned me about finning too hard near the bottom of the waters and stirring up the silt. As we approached the murky bottom of the lake, I grabbed hold of the frame of the open window of a bus and swung my feet around pointing my fins downwards (yes, I did say a bus – a big red one to be precise, sunk there for training purposes about fifteen metres down). Unfortunately, the momentum carried me down, until I was standing on the tips of my fins at the bottom, where the mud took hold and sucked one of my fins right off. I managed to struggle back up, and when I reported it to Ted he gave me a look that said I-told-you-so! No sooner had I told him than my fin started to surface within arms' length, much to his and my relief and I was able to put it back on, with a little help from him. We laughed a lot about it after, and I was subjected to a lot of teasing that evening in the bar, as everyone pictured me swimming round and round in circles. As for Ted, I think I really unnerved the poor guy; he seems to half expect me to do something silly. Don't get me wrong Ted is an excellent diver, with thousands of successful dives to his credit. Although seemingly unbothered by mundane things such as the weather, or if his dry-suit leaked like a teabag, or if he needed gloves when the water temperature dictated it, he was thoroughly professional under the pressure of safely bringing up a novice from a fairly deep dive, especially after an incident.

Fort Bovisand

I wrote this true story for our newsletter some time ago about a trip to Bovisand, because I thought it was quite amusing. In the summer of 1995, we went on a diving trip to Fort Bovisand. The diving rib was being towed by Ted and Christine, in their Range Rover and we followed behind. Driving down the M25 they slowed down as they approached major road works. They watched in disbelief as a wheel overtook them and rolled onto the opposite carriageway!
"Perhaps it's ours!" someone joked.
"Stop the car, it *is* ours!" cried Frank, and jumped out to retrieve it – not realising that it is illegal to cross the central reservation into the opposite carriageway. Before he had time to get back into the car, he was approached by an extremely irate patrolman, and had some explaining to do.
Luckily, the trailer was the two-axle type, because one of the wheel bearings had seized up, causing it to overheat and shear off the stub axle. I dread to think of the consequences if it had been a single axle trailer.

As we neared the end of our journey, up a steep winding lane that wended around the cliff face, we had the most hauntingly beautiful uninterrupted views over the harbour and the sea below us. Built into the cliff-face, near the top, was the large cobbled yard housing the magnificent Fort Bovisand Training Centre, renowned for its commercial and technical diver training.

From the glass-fronted gun-tower that housed the bar-restaurant, you'd be forgiven for thinking that your eyes were deceiving you, as down below, sticking out of the rock pools, bathed in gentle waves, the wreck of an 'N' reg VW Golf convertible shimmered under the light of the full moon.

Inside, the dark, dank, stone staircase led down to a labyrinth of long corridors containing the dormitories. Every couple of feet, the thick walls had been drilled with holes that led back up to the surface for ventilation. Although now patched over, these holes oozed rusty water that drip-dripped, echoing, into a wet puddle on the shiny flagstone floor. As you negotiated the eerie, dimly lit corridors at night on your way to the bathroom my imagination would run riot. Images of half-glimpses of Florence Nightingale disappearing into the distance, or of the mutilated soldier from a long-ago war, dripping blood from his open wounds, arms reaching out imploringly to grab you were enough to send me scurrying back to the stark, white-washed walls of the dormitory with its pre-war, cast-iron bunk-beds which reached almost to the ceiling. The high vaulted ceiling was criss-crossed from one side to the other with pipes and funnels, all covered in a thick layer of dust and cobwebs. We were awoken that night by an over-whelming smell of gas, as the room filled with smoke. As we tried to evacuate the room, one chap, still half asleep and dreaming tried to sweep the room with an imaginary broom, whilst swearing out orders to us, to get out of his way and let him finish his job. As we looked on and laughed we wondered about the merits of trying to wake him as we'd heard that it was dangerous to wake someone from a sleep-walking state, in this case sleep-working. We thought it might be fun to ask him to do the hall as well, which worked to our advantage as we got him out of the room without having to actually wake him up. After further investigation we found Frank's socks, firmly stuck to the red-hot radiator were the source of the gassy smell. His dry suit looked ready to burst into flames from the intense heat. There were red glowing embers falling from it as we moved the blackened material that was causing the acrid smoke. That could potentially have been a killer – it was lucky that I had awoken in the night to go to the toilet.

As I had the longer legs, I volunteered for the top bunk, enjoying too the sense of security knowing that hubby, Mike, was just beneath me. On entering the dorm one evening, we had noticed a little man with a close-shaven head who looked up at us with a cold stare in his eyes. He was kneeling by one of the bunks, unpacking his clothes from an old-fashioned brown leather suitcase, the type with shiny metal corner guards. From the top of the neat pile, he produced a pair of pyjamas. As he laid them out ready for bed, you could not help but notice the razor sharp creases pressed into the legs and arms. He was still unpacking long after Mike had read his newspaper and he and everyone else in the large dorm was trying to sleep, despite the cacophony of the snore-chorus that lasted from dusk till dawn. Have you ever had that feeling that you were being watched? Suddenly, I had the urge to open my eyes and to my horror, I was face-to-face with the little man, who was peering right into my face with those dark, dark eyes, close enough to kiss me. In shock, I looked on wide-eyed as he moved towards Mike and then on to some others in the room. As I recovered from my initial shock, I thought I had better say something, so I plucked up the courage to call;

"What do you think you're doing?"

This woke up Mike, who asked him the same question. Then the man had the cheek to ask *me* what *I* was doing!

"Trying to sleep, mate," was my reply. This seemed to annoy him.

"Who are you?" he asked. Now I was annoyed,

"Who are *you*?" I retorted. A long pause, and then in a voice that Norman Bates would have been proud of, he uttered,

"The caretaker!"

Finally, Mike (using his typical brand of abrupt diplomacy) told him in no uncertain terms where to go. So the moral of this story is, if you are diving up that way and you see someone you suspect to be the Creepy Caretaker, you will easily recognise him by the razor sharp creases in his dry suit.

My first holiday to the Red Sea.

On my first holiday to the Red Sea, I had my first night dive with John Sinclair on the Gobal Saghir. A great experience even though I was a little apprehensive at first. The torch lights helped light up the wreck and beyond and helped me relax into the dive where we saw a wide variety of different fish that you perhaps wouldn't see in the daytime. The next day on the thirteenth of November 1995, I passed the remainder of my sports diver test. We dived down to twenty-seven meters to a dive sight called Bluff Point and to my delight we saw some of the bigger pelagic. I found the current very heavy going on our way back so my dive instructor Barry Wingrave he told me to keep low and use the boulders to pull myself along the bottom until we got to a depth of about ten meters. Then Paul Young helped me to the surface where we swam to a small boat and I was able to get my breath back. From there Paul towed me to our day boat where once on board Kate Stafford made me a nice cup of hot sugary tea. Later I found out I was not the only one who had had a hard time, one of the guys even had to be rescued when he got swept away with the currant at the surface. That day on our afternoon dive, I gave John a buoyant life as part of my training and I was gobsmacked to learn later that I had gained the pass from our instructor Barry for my sports diver test. Before the next dive, Mike thought it would be funny to put a live fish into Christine Bonner's wet-suit. She felt it wriggling about and started to hop about screaming at the top of her voice as we all doubled up with laughter. She could not remove her suit quickly enough and fell about in her efforts to put her foot down, which made us laugh all the more. At five the next morning as we headed out on our boat, the sea conditions become treacherous and Joe Lloyd cracked a couple of ribs after being thrown across the boat as it hit wave after wave. Mike and John were being swept back and forth on their hands and knees whilst trying to stop the equipment boxes from floating through the opening at the back of the boat. Christine was screaming "turn the boat around we need to go back" but the craw were adamant it was better to carry on, while I propped myself up over the sink in the toilet cubical trying not to throw up. Everyone on the trip was wet through as water run down the walls soaking the floors above and below deck. Finally when we moored and the sea was calm enough for a strong cup of tea, we got to dive the much anticipated Thistlegorm. We waited at the top of the shot line for our dive guide Paddy to access the current and then we headed down the shot line and swam over to the top of the wreck. We went down inside the hold after our swim around the deck, where we saw a couple of land vehicle's and motor bikes, we also noticed that the deck was strewn with wellington boots. We managed to find the captain's quarters and I took a picture of Mike sitting in his bath. After a good look inside we explored a couple of the loco motive engines lying in the sand a few yards away, before swimming back to the shot line to decompress before coming up.

Sea-houses

In 1996, we dived several very different locations in quick succession over a few months. On 11th July we spent a long weekend at Stan Hall's bunkhouse in a place called Sea-houses, in the Farne Islands up in the North East of England.

The bunkrooms were simply furnished, but comfortable. The girls' dorm on the top floor of the house had several bunk beds lining the entire length of the room. Each bunk had its own pulley light switch, next to a nightstand. The advantage of sleeping on the top bunk, for me, was the nice view of the stars through the strategically placed Velux window in the ceiling. The men's bunkrooms were set out much the same, on the floor below ours. It was a bit of a trek each morning down three floors from the top of the house to the communal shower-room, situated on the cold concrete floor of the basement, at the bottom of a steep, dark stairwell.

Stan looked every bit the seafaring man, with his ruddy complexion and curly grey hair hanging just above his collar. His long straggly sideburns met a reddish brown beard, framing his firmly clenched tobacco-stained teeth that constantly clicked against his ceramic pipe as he spoke. He wore a thick knitted Aran-style wool jumper, with his trousers tucked neatly into his wellington boots. If it were raining when he was out in his boat, he'd wear a big yellow sou'wester over his woolly hat. In his spare time, he liked nothing more than to just tinker with boat engines and stuff that needed repair. He talked continually in a lovely soft Geordie accent about the loss of his brand new Renault Espace car, collected that day from the dealership in London. It was stolen from outside a shop in Ilford when he nipped inside for some tobacco.

Across from the bunkhouse, his house stood in a small cobbled courtyard. A small stable door opened into a large farmhouse-style breakfast room made snug and cosy with red gingham curtains hung at each window and a matching tablecloth and a wee posies of wild flowers placed on each table. This was Stan's wife's domain. She was a jolly lady with a full figure and a pleasant face, bidding you a good day with a nice smile for whoever entered her kitchen. Every morning before we left for our day's diving, a jug of fresh orange juice was placed on each table, followed by a large fried breakfast of sausages, eggs, mushrooms, tomatoes, black pudding, fried bread and beans. This was freshly cooked for you and followed by toast and jam if you wanted it, all washed down with numerous cups of tea.

Down the road from the lodgings was a nice bar with an outside restaurant where we could chill out with a beer and eat our suppers in the pretty gardens, before sunset. At the other end of the road a couple of shops overlooked the village green and one of them was a take-away fish and chips shop. The day we were due to leave we decided to nip down to the 'chippy' for lunch, which we ate in the car with little wooden forks. The large white polystyrene container absolutely over-flowed with large, fat chips and freshly caught that morning, the biggest, tastiest piece of battered cod, smothered in salt and vinegar all washed down with a steaming hot cup of tea. There weren't much else to see in this part of Sea-houses, just the local pub around the corner and the rows of terraced houses with their pretty walled gardens built from the local stone.

The Chris Christianson and the SS Somali

Most days, we went out on Stan's boat, The Farne Diver and the diving was excellent. We dived on a couple of good wrecks. The visibility was very good on the Chris Christianson, but the SS Somali of Glasgow – all that remained of her was her spine, but we managed to dig out loads of old Bovril jars. I didn't realise that Bovril was that old. It was also great fun to swim in the strong current through the thick, wavering kelp beds, even though it did make me feel queasy at times. The deep gullies that lay in long lines between the kelp beds were filled with different coloured starfish in various shapes and sizes and giant spider crabs that would reach up to grab you as you glided over them. We saw a pair doing battle on a sandy part of the seabed. It was like watching something from 'Star Wars'. Their smaller pincers were constantly prodding and thrusting like small light sabres, whilst they held their larger claw pincer high over their heads behind them, in a kind of duelling stance, ready for the kill. There was an abundance of the so-called 'dead man's fingers' which caused you to give them a double take as you swam by because that's exactly what they look like. On closer inspection though, they were all soft and squiggly and looked more like blown up white rubber gloves.

One day during the week we went out on the rib to a place called Blue Caps to swim with the seals that colonized the rocks there. It was a totally amazing experience. Some of the seals were quite friendly, and we even managed to lie down with some of the mothers and their pups, on the smooth shelving submerged about ten metres down. Some of the juvenile seals were very curious and darted about in front of us. One even came right up to the camera, putting his nose on it whilst trying to bite it. On the way up from the dive one of them tried to get me to play with him by hanging on to my fin. I was feeling a bit queasy from the constant sway of the kelp and the large swell of the water pitching me up and down. So Mike, bless him, gave me a buoyant lift to the surface – after all, isn't that what buddies are for. I suppose you could say that it was fortunate that we were still in water because I found I could no longer contain the feeling of sickness and as I took out my mouthpiece to say thanks, a huge projectile of vomit came hurtling out of my mouth, narrowly missing his face.

Mike had managed to get a good picture of the seal and its antics with my fins and it won the annual photo competition for that year. So with pride and joy we see his framed picture hanging on the clubhouse wall, amongst the winners from previous years.

The Riversdale, Salcombe

Ted took me on my first really deep dive on a week's holiday in July 1996 off the coast of Salcombe in Devon, a natural progression in our training, but perhaps a little deep for someone with so little experience. The sea around these parts is a beautiful emerald green, with fair to good visibility that makes for very good diving. There are plenty of good wrecks, including the Riversdale, which was sunk at about forty-five metres. Our brief that morning, guided by our GPS, was to dive down to the wreck, swim around the top of it for a few minutes and then ascend slowly up Ted's delayed SMB (submerged buoyancy aid). But that's not quite what happened! For a start, the current must have taken our shot line further out than the GPS had predicted, leaving it just short of the wreck, so a short swim was necessary. But I just could not swim to it and I quickly got out of breath after a couple of strokes. Twice more we tried and then I made the mistake of gesturing to Ted with my mouthpiece that I was breathless. Then I made a signal with my fingers that I wanted to go up a short way to see if it would ease the situation. But Ted misread my signals and thought that I was indicating a problem with my air supply. He checked my air gauges, which appeared to be functioning as normal, so decided that I probably meant that I needed to get up fast. He started to fill my jacket with air, and before I could indicate that I was all right he had inflated my dry-suit as well. There is a condition in deep diving called nitrogen narcosis, which makes thinking difficult - divers call it 'getting narked'. Anyway, he also inflated his own jacket, and we shot to the surface as if rocket-propelled. I think Ted was intent on getting me up on my own steam for a time but changed his mind as we lifted from the seabed. There had been an incident on the same wreck recently, when a diver died, after getting separated from his dive buddies. That could explain why Ted filled his own jacket straight after filling mine, because he thought he might lose me on the way up. I'll never know for sure because he doesn't remember all the details – a sure sign of narcosis.

Back on board, we were given oxygen for a few hours. After a once-over from the coxswain, were deemed fit by the time we got back to shore. As we had been in the water for only a few minutes, it was considered a bounce dive, and there was no evidence of nitrogen build-up, so we were fortunate on this occasion.

Early one morning we dived for scallops and I made fantastic paella for our evening meal. I was very proud of the final result and especially pleased with the comments I received at dinner. They all said it tasted every bit as authentic as the paella you order from a Spanish restaurant. On a previous dive trip, another dive buddy, Tina Hards 'may she rest in peace', taught us the correct way to open and clean scallops, which came in handy for my paella. It was something she had picked up whilst training as a marine biologist and found it to be quite economical, served with rice and vegetables. You lightly fry a couple of finely chopped garlic cloves in a knob of best butter, add the scallops and salt and pepper to taste. Wrap them in foil and cook on the BBQ. Include the gonads, as she called them (the reproductive parts to you and me) as they are tasty as well as extremely nutritious.

Another of the girls on board, Tess and her friend Tom went out fishing that morning and caught a couple of sea bass. After they prepared them for our BBQ we included them with our meal and they were just as delicious.

We took off for a swim that evening with a couple of basking sharks, which frequent the bay at that time of year. I was lucky enough to swim an arm's length away from a fifteen-footer. I was completely in awe of his huge body and his fin that with one fell swoop could have knocked me clean out of his way. It was exhilarating to say the least, to swim alongside this giant pelagic, more than twice my length but as gentle as a kitten. It felt pretty strange and perhaps a little scary, as it possibly was for him, too. As he held me in his stare, I was mesmerised by that big, sad-looking eye staring back so intensely. I danced about, trying to keep my buoyancy, with one arm stretched out as high above water level as I could, making an OK signal with my hand to let the others know where he was. It seemed to me that he had the hint of a smile and purposely kept his mouth closed so as to get a clear view of me. They filter tons of krill to feed on, with their enormous mouths wide open, which makes it hard for them to see.

One evening we took a trip a couple of miles upstream to a pub in Kingsbridge on the tender, a small boat we could use to make it easier to get around. Ted (or Jonah as we also referred to him) managed to run aground and bent the skeg (the gear casing) in the process. As we had only journeyed for a short way downstream, he decided to turn back to try to fix it. As we fast approached the jetty, we heard a familiar voice screaming out at us and realised that it was Tessa in floods of tears. We had accidently left her behind and we never heard the last of it all the following week. She thought we had left her behind for a laugh, but in truth it was because we left in haste in order to get back again before dark. But it was still funny!

We had a great time, and lots of fun that week. You cannot imagine what a great thrill it is in a rib full to its capacity with divers yet plaining across the water still snug in your dry-suit and not caring what the weather threw at you.

Lundy Island and the Carmen Filomena

On 9th August 1996, we spent another long weekend diving around Lundy Island, in the Bristol Channel. The boat was called The Datchet and was all right if you didn't have misgivings about the skipper, Dave. He served your breakfast bacon straight from the frying pan with his yellow, tobacco stained fingers, accompanied by large, cylindrical lumps of cigarette ash which dropped from the permanent fixture stuck between his lips. And sharing the showers and toilet facilities with a dozen men, who left the seat in a permanently upright position! Several wet bottoms later, I figured that if I wanted to use the facilities in the dark, I needed to bring a torch. It also helps to prevent disturbing the other sleepers in the darkened corridor of coffin-style bunk beds, stacked floor to ceiling. With just a curtain across the front, any privacy goes straight out of the window. Not to mention the constant barrage of beer-induced wind ejected from both ends of the men. And the rippling chorus of snores that kept me awake till the wee, small hours. But when all's said and done, it was somewhere cosy to rest my head at the end of a hard day's diving and to me adds to the fun of it all.

Lundy Island is a stunning carpet of rich green velvet rock, poking out of the emerald green sea. Dave would take us ashore in the tender, after diving. We'd embark onto a sand and pebble beach, strewn with driftwood and the like. We then had an arduous climb up the side of the windswept cliff, on a path formed by rocks, moulded under foot, to form a smooth set of stairs. At the top we reached the most welcoming sight of the bar restaurant, where we were entertained by a DJ over our meal and beverage, while mulling over the day's diving.

For the adventurous, there are long, bracing walks around the Island, and up to the peak to take in the breathtakingly beautiful views and to enjoy the tangled mat of pretty wild-flowers tumbling through the lush undergrowth, awash with salty sea-spray. Here too are a number of crumbling follies, where stately homes once stood, now locked behind tall, ivy-encrusted rusty railings.

As you head down from the peak, the steep, well-worn pathways, held back by felled logs, give way to a grassy plateau near the bottom. A long, winding wall, built entirely from the shale rock set into cement, encloses a pen for sheep and a number of out buildings together with a barn. For me, best of all were the puffins! They seemed oblivious of us, waddling past with their deep-set eyes and thick, toucan-style beaks. They nested up on the cold, hard rock face, under the shelter of the overhanging canopy, their calls echoing out to the sea.
The diving wasn't half bad, either.

We dived a couple of wrecks on the first day and the beautiful Seals Rock which was also another very interesting dive with lots of giant burgundy fan-coral and monster sea cucumbers creeping all over an array of colourful jewel anemone.

The wreck of the Carmen Filomena, although old and broken into large pieces around its perimeter, still held a lot of interest to poke around in, with deep gullies that brimmed with starfish and giant spider crabs.

Whilst kitting up for one of the dives, for a laugh Mike decided to place a couple of raw eggs into Eddie's dry suit since he was always amongst the missing when it came to a bit of extra work. It went unnoticed until Mike suddenly yelped 'oh no' and held up a large piece of congealed egg as he proceeded to peel it from inside his suit. From experience he always wore plastic bags over his socks to keep his feet warm and dry, so the eggs formed a solid mass around the plastic bag from the heat of his body. We were extremely amused all evening with the banter and variations of the egg sandwich jokes! What made it even funnier was apart from Mike smelling eggier than his usual self was

Eddie's unawareness that the egg was really meant for him because his suit was identical to Mikes!

Shoreham – Looe Gate Reef and the Stanoola

A couple of weeks later, in September, we popped down to Shoreham in Sussex where we hired a boat for the weekend. The skipper was a very unsavoury type, covered from head to toe in pus-filled green spots that were most evident even through his grubby vest top. His smoke-stained green teeth clenched a fag butt the entire time, and looked like they hadn't seen a toothbrush in years. By the state of his nicotine-stained fingers, with nails that were bitten right down to the quick, you certainly wouldn't want him serving up your breakfast on any account. But his heart was in the right place, he made us all feel very welcome, with cups of hot tea and biscuits after each dive, and he would take us anywhere we wanted.

We had an excellent dive, with good visibility on a small gunboat wreck, then onto Looe Gate Reef. It was very pretty, with sandy banks but the swell made me feel sick. By the time we got to the surface, coming up by my delayed submerged buoyancy aid (SMB for short) I had a bad nosebleed and was heaving once again. I also managed to get wet through on the last dive of the week on the wreck of the Stanoola, as my neck seal had slightly perished, letting in bucket loads of water, soaking me right down to my boots. Still, the weather was nice all weekend, and I managed to grab a few rays of sunshine to warm up.

Puerto Del Carmen – Red Cross Reef

During November, we spent a week's holiday in Puerto Del Carmen in Lanzarote. We hired a couple of cars to get us all down to the beach. The dive school was very good, taking us out to many of the good reefs, and if we had enough air left after our day's diving, we used it to dive in the bay that evening. We had a couple of nice dives just off the beach, after wading out from the rocky shore. On one reef, in the middle of the bay I managed to use my compass to great effect. There were lots of different fish, including a jet-black tang, edged in electric blue, which tried its best to get into my mask. You have to be very careful with them as they have a sharp blade near their tail. Typically, when I tried to take a picture, my camera wouldn't flash. Mike chopped up a black spiked sea urchin to feed to the other fish, which ate the lot in a frenzy of jutting teeth and bubbles. They are breeding so fast there that there is a danger of them taking over the bay and depleting the coral completely.

I had my second night dive in the bay with Tony Crowhurst, one of the guys in our party. I was a bit apprehensive at first, but I needn't have worried so much as it was not that dark. Even when you turned off your torch, you could still see your way around the rocks by the light of the moon. There was an abundance of colourful nightlife that you don't see in the daytime, including an octopus that changed colour several times as it swam by. Several cuttlefish were drawn by the light of our torches. They had big, sad-looking eyes that followed your every move, and they darted in and out of the torchlight like jet-propelled darts.

A few minutes' walk up the beach, not far off shore, there are three boats sunk at about fifteen metres almost on top of each other. It is an amazing sight and as you approach the first one, you can see the second and then the third quite clearly. About five years later they sunk two more ships in the same vicinity. If you are good on air, you can dive them all one after the other by starting at the deepest first, which lies at about thirty five metres; then by the time you get to the shallowest you are well into decompression. We also had a couple of deep dives off the rib. The visibility was excellent, and I logged the Red Cross Reef as the best dive of the week. I think it was because we saw a giant grouper, and an even larger angel shark sunning itself in the sand. It shot off into the distance when Mike pulled its tail. We also saw an even bigger octopus keeping its eye on us as he camouflaged himself to blend in with his surroundings. A large shoal of barracuda swam quite close overhead, and we were even more ecstatic when we saw Sharon and Paul playing with a giant manta ray. It seemed to be having great fun, gliding right over their heads as they stroked it, and it circled back to them for another go. I was disappointed that it had finished its game by the time we got to them, but I managed to get a really good picture this time.

The last time we were there, we noticed something very amusing whilst snorkelling around the edge of the bay. Just along the seawall, there are lots of interesting fish, as well as lots of angel sharks. They bury themselves just under the surface of the sand in the shallow parts of the warm water. You have to laugh when you see an unsuspecting tourist wading out and then suddenly letting out a scream and hopping about, trying to get out of the water as fast as possible when they realise that it's a shark that they have accidently trodden on.

The Maldives

1997 was just as exciting. In April, for our 25th Wedding Anniversary, we took ourselves off to the Maldives. After a twelve-hour flight, only stopping on the way at Bahrain, we finally touched down in Mali. From there, we continued the rest of our journey over sea south of the Atoll, by speedboat, until we finally reached the island of Eriyadu. A tiny Island, no bigger than two football pitches Eriyadu is set in azure seas with a pure white sandy beach that reached almost to our thatched-roofed condo.

The swaying coconut palms were strung together with colourful hammocks, where you could chill out swinging in the breeze, amongst the colourful flora of the lush, tropical gardens that grew along the water's edge.

A triggerfish used to meet us in the bay every morning, waiting to be fed. We were warned that they can be quite dangerous, but we saved our breakfast bread crusts for him, not realising that he could have taken off our fingers in one bite!

We were not at all impressed with the diving school, though. They put us through an unnecessary dive test, God knows why! If they had looked at our dive logs, which are a prerequisite when diving with BSAC, they would have realised that we probably had more dives under our belts than most of their dive guides. Diving back home in England in a dry-suit is a darn sight harder, when the visibility can be only eight to ten feet if you are lucky, on a good day. Plus, the dives priced at £30 a time were a little excessive. We ended up booking a small dive package, costing about £175 for two dives a day over five days. These could be taken as and when we liked over the next two weeks. This left us with lots of time to chill out and do a bit of snorkelling. We discovered that the perimeter of the Island's house reef was teeming with life.

One particular time, whilst out snorkelling, we were so engrossed that we didn't notice that the current had taken us to the far side of the reef. We had been told that this area would not hold much interest because the coral had died right back due to the El Niño (warming of the sea). How wrong can you be? Even though it has had a devastating effect on the reef, which now resembles a bone yard, the most amazing things happened there that afternoon. Not only did we get our first ever real close up of a white-tipped reef shark, who eyed us menacingly as though trying to decide whether or not we looked like lunch. He swam alarmingly close, as we hugged close to the reef. But there, swimming just below us, was a giant moray eel, all eight to twelve feet of him, presumably also looking for his lunch. And gathering at the edge of the reef a whirling shoal of extremely large jacks swam in ever-increasing circles. With nowhere else to go, Mike started to slowly slip the camera from around his neck to use as a weapon. But no sooner had he done so, thank goodness the shark must have thought better of it, or something gave him a fright as he gave us another quick buzz, before disappearing at full speed, off into the distance.

You might think that this kind of experience would be enough to put us off diving for good, but I can honestly say that it only adds to the thrill of it. I was not frightened by the experience at the time, and it was only after discussing it at length over dinner that we decided that we had had a narrow escape.

After dinner we'd stroll along the fully illuminated jetty, looking at all the fish drawn to the underwater lights. There we'd sit and chill out, along with all the other couples, and maybe count the many needlefish. One very hot evening, after a couple of beers in the Moldavian style bar, we strolled down the jetty as usual, but this time, on our way, we spotted a couple of nurse sharks, swimming in and out under the walk-way. Mike decided he would like to join them, and as there were a lot of people sitting there, cooling off, we decided to walk right to the end of the long jetty. There, without warning, Mike suddenly disappeared off the end, making the biggest almighty dive bomb he could muster. He hit the sea at full throttle, totally soaking every one with a giant wave that travelled more than half the length of the jetty. It was the funniest thing, seeing all those people in all their finery, one minute just sitting there dangling their feet in the warm water and the next soaked through by a tidal wave. It smacked against them, whilst simultaneously sending a barrage of needlefish flying through the air. As they rained down onto the deck, they made a loud slapping sound all around us. Still, it cooled everyone down!

Baltimore – The Kowloon Bridge

In July of that year we also had a week in Baltimore, on the coast of Ireland. The accommodation was quite nice. The small chalet type bungalow had beautiful views across open fields on one side, and boats of all kinds sitting in the slimy mud of the estuary on the other, Mike's brother, Larry, and his wife Margaret paid us a visit at the beginning of our week there. They had quite a long journey to get to us from a rain-soaked Cork city where they lived. The weather was good to them that day and they had a great time.

We visited the town of Baltimore and ate in a pub-restaurant that evening. In general we've always found the food to be quite good in Ireland, and the Irish people generous with their portions with hart warming puddings like sticky toffee pudding and custard, and apple-pie with ice-cream. After we had eaten our fill, we took a long walk around the picturesque harbour, with its many shops and restaurants. As we approached the bottom of the hill, we could hear loud shouting coming from the top, and people started to run down towards us with what looked like a ball. It was in fact a 2lb. steel ball which is used for the game of Boules – it is rolled downhill to see who can get it the furthest. Mike immediately recognized it as being a game he used to play as a kid. So he asked one of the guys in the group if he knew of a chap called Laddie Coade, who played this weird but exciting game. The guy said he did know him, but he was on the other team. He would leave word with someone at the pub that we were looking for him. Lo and behold, what a small world we live in – it turns out that Laddie was there, and he's one of the cousins that Larry used to play with as a child. They had not seen each other since Mike left Ireland as a young lad.

One evening, one of our chaps, Chris Mills, decided to cook us all a fish supper, accompanied by an assortment of spicy vegetables. His wife is from Belize and they tended to eat a lot of fish. He said that he was sure he could replicate one of her nice dishes, as he had helped her to cook many times. Although it had been in the fridge for quite some time, when he attempted to gut the Pollock, it started to jump about. Chris screamed in terror. We were all taken aback by his screaming and jumping about, but just could not stop laughing. I don't think his wife would have been too impressed either, if she had seen the mess he made with all the preparations. The place was a bit crowded and with twenty or so of us crowded around the kitchen table; it made it look a lot worse. But after we had calmed him down we all had a good laugh and the meal turned out fine.

Luckily for us, the weather was quite good that week. The diving there can be quite rough at times, with high winds, big choppy seas and exceptionally strong currents. The skipper of The Girl Sharon decided to take us out on the first day's diving, even though the waves were quite high (white horses we call them) and most of the other boats would not leave the safety of the harbour. The diving was still quite good though with fair visibility most of the time. On one of our last dives of the day, I felt a bit nauseous coming up the ladder. Dave Blaxland asked me if I was all right, but the moment I stepped onto the boat another wave of nausea overcame me. So I answered Dave with my hand half-covering my mouth, in case it was just trapped wind. In that instant, what I thought was just a burp was indeed vomit that filled my hand as it forced its way out between my fingers catching Dave full in the face. After my initial embarrassment we had a good laugh about it for the rest of the evening. But worse was yet to come! The next day, after getting into his dive kit, Dave ran through his buddy checklist, and naturally put his regulator into his mouth to check that his air supply was flowing freely. Instead, he found himself with a mouthful of carrots and stuff from yesterday's vomit.

That evening, he must have scrubbed his mouth out a dozen times with a toothbrush and a whole tube of toothpaste. He found it very hard to talk about it without retching and turning a shade of green. You can imagine the constant ribbing he had to put up with for the rest of the week, whilst we fell about with laughter at the mere mention of it.

We also dived in the S.W. of Point Cape Clear. Mike had a bit of a problem and he started to rise on the way down. His wrist dump valve would not dump the excess air you put in your drysuit to stop you getting squeezed from the ambient pressure. He asked me to hold on to him while he tried to dump the air from the cuff on his sleeve. But every time he tried he had visions of getting soaked and stopped himself short. He even held his arm out at one point and gestured to me to do it. As I grabbed his sleeve, he kept pulling away, and we started to go upwards at an alarming rate. We had gone from thirty metres to fifteen in a matter of seconds, as I held on to him for dear life before he remembered to bring his knees up to his chest. In this scrunched up position, the air came flooding out of his neck seal, and we grabbed at the shelving sticking out of the wall in an effort to slow ourselves down. As we came to a halt, we came face-to-face with a small shark that was as shocked to see us as we were to see him. After the dive, I asked Mike about his reluctance to let me pull his cuff, and he admitted that he didn't fancy getting a soaking. I said, "You would have preferred the bends, then?" In all our years of diving that's the first time we have come pretty close to missing our decompression stops.

Also something quite astonishing occurred on one of the wreck dives that week. After what seemed like a very long and uneventful swim at about fifteen metres, looking all the time for the wreck of the Kowloon Bridge. We suddenly came across a solid wall, rising up out of nowhere, and immediately we realised that we had been swimming in the hold of the ship all along! At a staggering 150,000 tons, it is one of the biggest ships we have ever been fortunate to dive in around Europe. It was totally empty, apart for a lot of loose shot scattered around the solid steal floor of the hold. As there was not much else to see, we decided to inspect her hull, and swam down over her side for a further 15 metres or more. It was a sight to be seen – the whole of the side of the hull was completely covered in colourful anemone and deathly white 'dead man's fingers'.

I lost Mike coming back up, somehow we missed each other and I was not very pleased about it. You must never lose sight of your buddy and to come up without them is unthinkable. I was very concerned for his safety and decided to do what any other diver would do. I swam back, glancing over the top of the deck as far as I could see. But I had only a limited amount of air, and had to abandon my search after a couple of minutes and return to the shot line to finish my decompression. I worried constantly whilst doing my compression stops if he had made it back to the surface all right! You can imagine my surprise when I climbed back into the boat, with a thumping head, and saw him happily polishing off a hot cup of tea. He said that he could see my bubbles rising so he knew I was on the shot below him, but what he never knew was how much it had scared me!

Eilat – The Sateen, and Taba

In November of that year, we managed to cram in another week's holiday, and this time we chose Eilat, in Israel, on the northern tip of the Red Sea. It is one of our most memorable trips ever.

Even though it was not the deal that he thought he had booked, Mike, in his haste hadn't noticed that it was a *hostel*, and went ahead and booked what he thought was a hotel. We didn't suspect it until we arrived and were greeted by a very irate Israeli guy who immediately tried to confiscate our armfuls of duty-free alcohol. He also refused to let us into our rooms unless we agreed not to consume it on his premises. As we couldn't be seen walking around town with our booze and one of the guys had brought a music centre with him; we came to the conclusion that the only solution was to have a party on the patio outside. This was a huge mistake, it seemed to wind up the hostel owner even more, and instead of going home to his bed, he decided to sleep in his office where he could keep an eye on us.

Every ten minutes or so he would come out to turn the music down, until in the end it was so low that we could hardly hear it, so in retaliation we'd turn it back up a little. This went on for a couple of hours, until, in a huff, he turned it off completely. He then refused point-blank to let us back into our rooms. After a heated debate about our cases and stuff, he finally conceded when we pointed out that the room he had billed as a 'single room' was in fact a long broom-cupboard a bucket's width across at the far end, with a mattress on the floor. Anything other than sleep was out of the question as all the couples in the party had to share their double beds overlooked by two or three bunk beds. John and Jill decided to share the broom-cupboard, with their feet at the bucket end. It was extremely uncomfortable and impossible to sleep in a straight line. Also as it was a hostel, the double rooms only had a large wardrobe between the four or five people sharing the room. As you can imagine, by the end of the week they looked more like the local launderette, strewn with wet towels and washing hanging from every bed-post and in every available space.

Mike and I were the lucky ones and had a double bed in our own small room. John and Jill of the broom-cupboard were able to hang some of their clothes in our room. I suppose as most of the rooms were really meant for backpackers, which had not been mentioned at the time of booking, we decided to make use of what we had, rather than trying to find somewhere else able to accommodate us all at such short notice. Never the less, we had a great laugh and two of our diving party got together after they each decided to sleep on the patio one night where it was less crowded and a lot cooler. They have since wed.

Every night we would go into town to suss out the nightlife in the local bars. One night we ended up in a disco, and as a group we danced the night away with each other's partners. The funny thing was when several times I turned down a guy who had asked me to dance and when he asked me why not, since I had danced with everyone else! I told him we were all friends, and part of a group on a diving holiday. It must have looked like great fun to outsiders, as they kept asking if they could join us. We got a little bit boisterous as the night wore on, and as a bet all twenty-four of us tried to sit on the same chair. The chair-legs buckled under our weight and we all ended up laughing in a heap in the middle of the dance floor.

As you can imagine, some of us were a bit the worst for wear in the morning. So for ease of diving, we booked a dive with dolphins in a national park environment. I must admit I didn't quite know what to expect, and was a little disappointed, as were the rest of the group, with the bad visibility in the seawater enclosures. But the giant fan coral gardens, harbouring a reef of brightly coloured fish, around a man-made folly resembling the lost city of Atlantis was quite impressive. As was the sunken pirate ship with treasure chests spilling out their precious contents among the ruins, and a scattering of 'booty' spread about the outskirts for us to swim over. A bit further along, we were asked to kneel in rows on the sandy seabed as the dolphins zipped in and out between us, which was quite exhilarating. As I was at the back, I was a little annoyed when we were told to swim on every time I knelt up straight to get a better view of the dolphins juggling hoops and rings to one another. Luckily I had a better view for the more spectacular tricks, just before the end of the dive.

One of the guides leading the dive lay on his back and blew enormous oxygen/water rings from his mouth, like giant smoke rings. Then by blowing oxygen into the mouth of one of the dolphins, it was able to mimic him by blowing its own rings to the other dolphins, waiting patiently in line ready to catch them over their noses. If you sat quite still they would come right up to you and kiss your cheek, then disappear as quickly as they came. Even though they looked healthy, and they seemed to enjoy it, I was a little concerned as they were in captivity, and you couldn't help feeling that they would be better off in their own environment.

We dived some really good wrecks throughout the week, and we managed to do a training dive at the beginning. We had a good dive with fair visibility on the wreck of the Sateen, where I mimicked climbing the ship's stairs one fin after the other, making everyone behind me laugh.

But by the end of the week, we had had enough of the poor visibility and decided to take a trip over to Taba in Egypt. Whilst on our first dive of the day, we accidently crossed the border back into Eilat. A couple of the lads crossed the invisible line underwater, noted by a submarine no less. The authorities were straight onto us, and arrived at the dive-school toting their guns casually thrown over their shoulders. They demanded that we abandon the day's diving so that they could check the infiltrators' passports and visas. We spent the rest of the day waiting around at the dive-school where, at one point, they even threatened to hold one of the lads indefinitely, as he had lost his visa. Luckily for him one of our guys found it, and they decided to let him leave with us.

It was a total relief at the border into Israel, with its familiar surroundings and the friendly smiling faces of the Israelis, dressed in their crisp cotton shirts and lightweight uniforms. Unfortunately, the relief was cut short all too soon by the oppressive regime in the place we had to return to. With all the solemn faces of the staff at Passport Control, decked out in their heavy navy blue uniforms, and the women wearing long, black, military-style burkas from head to toe, alongside the gun-toting guards, it was a very hot, inhospitable environment.

La Cave des Tuileries

In July 1998, we took a week-long trip to Marseilles, in Southern France, to dive at La Cave des Tuileries. Our accommodation was a ferry boat conversion called 'Ocean Passage', originally out of the Bay of Biscay.

A varnished, dark-oak handrail led down a wide, open-plan stairwell, where a large leather sofa, with an adjacent coffee table strewn with dive magazines, occupied a cosy space beneath. A TV set firmly fixed into a cabinet against the wall at one end of the room faced the washrooms at the other in a corridor with several doors leading to our bedrooms, thus creating a very comfortable lounge area. Some of the bedrooms had bunks for several single people sharing and others a small double bed for couples.

A blue handrail around the perimeter of the boat gave a clear, uninterrupted view across the beautiful bay, like an infinity pool, with far-reaching views over the rocky headland beyond, gently tapering at either end into the surrounding azure blue sea.
We gathered on deck for our evening meal, around a couple of long dining tables which had been set out with crisp, white tablecloths and large candles in sturdy holders. After dinner, late into the evening, we'd gossip about the good old days, as we sipped a glass or two of wine and watched the kids having fun on the white sandy beach across the bay. The bronzed bodies of the jet-skiers whizzed up and down the bay till late in the evening. As the sun went down we were privy to some of the most amazing sunsets that reddened the sky like an out-of-control fire across the horizon, signalling time for bed, with an early start in the morning.
We had a go at water surfing from the back of our own little tender, although we got a telling-off from the beach patrol for practising too near the beach. Getting the hang of standing up was quite difficult but, to the disappointment of several of the

others who were too heavy for the little ten-horsepower engine, a few of us including Jen, managed to master it, and I thoroughly enjoyed the experience.

I was full of apprehension after the brief, about La Caves des Tuileries, but my apprehension turned to elation as they were easily accessible and extremely pretty once inside. The stalactites and stalagmites looked absolutely awesome, engulfed in torchlight casting eerie shadows above and beyond our surreal surroundings. We lay on our backs and lazily drifted along aimlessly with the pull of the current. After what seemed like an eternity, but probably no more than twenty minutes or so, we neared the end of this cave, where we had to duck-dive down and up, into another smaller chamber. It was a bit of a tight squeeze to accommodate us all, but it was equally as breath-taking and incredibly it was full of breathable air. As we sat there, gathered around the edge of the rocks, admiring the formations above water level, our instructor showed us a truly magical phenomenon, the aptly named bioluminescence. With the vigorous wave of his hand, just below the water's surface, an astonishing, magnificent glow appeared. Apparently, this luminescence is all around us in the sea, yet only visible to the naked eye in the dark. As we swam back down and out of that chamber and into another larger one, we practised the hand-waving technique a couple of times, to see for ourselves if it really worked. Then we continued on down, into the depths of the cave, until we reached the seabed below. We headed back towards our exit, a beacon of hazy, green, shimmering light from the sun's intense rays shining down through the mouth of the cave, some eighteen metres above.

A foaming, frothy bib of white sand and an azure blue sea, gently lapping at the bottom of a rocky white cliff was our chosen place of shelter for the night. Moored up alongside us was a dazzling array of smaller boats, in their individual splendour. The other coves that we stayed overnight in that week all had the same beautiful appearance, especially in the early morning sunshine. Except for one where, on further inspection aided by a pair of binoculars, you could plainly see a cage of iron bars covering the windows of a dungeon, dug out of the sandstone of the cliff face. Our skipper, Neal, told us that this is one of the places where they quarantined everyone coming over from England, to keep the plague at bay.

Further up the coast, in another equally pretty bay we dived that morning, we found some mosaic floor tiles scattered about on the seabed. Naturally, we thought we had found a treasure trove. But we were disappointed to find out later that they were left over from the film set of the fictitious palace of the Count of Monte Christo. Still, they would have been a good find for someone who was a bit of a film buff.

Le Lavandou, Southern France

We dived again in France in June 1999, in a place called Toulon in Le Lavandou, Southern France. The hire boat for that week had a serious problem that Walter, our Skipper, seemed unable to fix himself, at such short notice anyway. We all had thoughts of being marooned at port for a couple of days, while she underwent repairs, and being fed on heaps of sauerkraut, which we found out, was the norm for the rest of the week. So after a bit of cajoling from Mike, Ray was able to bluff his way down into Walter's engine room to take an informative look at her generator. As Ray suspected, here was the problem. He took some of its parts to bits, thoroughly cleaned them, and then miraculously put them back together again. I say miraculously because he confessed that he was not sure how he managed to fit it all together, in the right place, and have it up and running at his first attempt. We were very grateful to Ray, with his 'limited knowledge' as it is not the first time that he has been able to get us out of a bit of bother with broken engines and the-like. I remember another time when he 'managed' to fix an air compressor whilst on a livaboard in the Red Sea. We would have been limited in our choice of diving and, as seasoned divers we expected to go further afield.

So, with much relief all round, we were able to set sail for our week's diving in Toulon the following morning, but not before Walter's dog had hopped off to do his morning business. To me, it seems a strange way of life for a dog. You can just imagine the poor animal having to cross his legs until the next port of call. But he seemed to manage it quite well, and only had a couple of 'accidents' on deck that I know of. On both occasions they were quickly washed away with a splash of disinfectant and a bucket of soapy water. It seemed like a complete accident to us all, as he could see land and wagged his tail in anticipation and with extreme excitement as we neared it.

Port de Tort and the Spahis

That week we had the pleasure of diving a site called Port de Tort and got our first ever real close-up look at a tiny little seahorse, in quite a stunning rusty-red colour, clinging by its long tail, in a mirror image of its surroundings a profusion of red berry-like growths, growing amongst the tall grasses. I was totally thrilled to bits at getting a better look at its wonderful horse-shaped head and flaring nostrils, when it suddenly, very gracefully moved, uncurling its long tail as it grasped for another hold in its place of refuge. I promised myself, there and then, that I would buy myself a better camera, one with a built-in macro lens.

We dived on the wreck of the Spahis that afternoon, but the lack of interest and fish-life led us to look further afield, where we came across a large octopus. Frank Turner, one of the guys diving alongside us, reckoned that they are very intelligent creatures and apparently he kept one as a pet in an aquarium at home. He told us that if you placed a meal in a large screw-capped jar in the aquarium, they would unscrew the lid in a matter of minutes. So when we came across this really big one, heading for the nearest shelter as soon as it saw us, it didn't dent Frank's bravado in the slightest. He plunged headfirst, one arm outstretched deep into the octopus's bolt-hole, and grabbed at it in the dark crevice. I didn't want him to pull it out on my behalf, and laughed under my breath when suddenly Frank lurched forward onto his knees. With a determined show of brute force, to my utter and total disbelief when he pulled his arm out, he was still in possession of one of the octopus's twitching tentacles which had wound itself around his arm. He peeled it off, and I told him off using underwater sign language as he proceeded to chase me through the gullies, waving the wriggling tentacle at me, throughout the rest of the dive. As I climbed the ladder, he held it over my head, all the time taunting me with it. Once on board, he could see that I was more annoyed than frightened, as he jiggled it in front of my face. He tried to pacify me by saying that the tentacle would grow back in a matter of months. I don't know if that is true or not, but my initial shock and horror of his action made me vow never to talk to him ever again. I must admit that I mellowed a little later on towards the end of the week. After a lot of ribbing from him and from the others, I had to laugh in the end, because it must have seemed quite funny to any onlookers.

Cherbourg – The Strathblane and SS Ousso

The following year, on 6th August 2000, we hired a boat out of Weymouth Harbour, called 'The White Horse', for our third trip across the English Channel. This time we went to Cherbourg, then over to Normandy to dive Omaha Beach, where the D-Day landings took place. I considered this, to be the trip of a lifetime, and I'm glad the opportunity arose for us to dive there, but it turned out to be an exceptionally emotional week for me.

Every evening we'd moor the boat in the prettiest of bays, tucked away from the wind and the harsher weather coming in off the open sea. After a leisurely meal, we'd all chill out with a drink and enjoy a real sense of camaraderie. We'd listen intently whilst the older guys in our group conversed about their former years with extraordinary stories that usually involved a villain or two, amongst other things. One intriguing story was about a very enterprising young man, who shall remain anonymous, after he ended up in prison, unable to realise his fortune. He supposedly invented the B.C.D. (buoyancy control device), or stab jacket as they are referred to now. But it was patented by someone else whilst he was away, and the rest is history. I can't elaborate further, I don't fancy ending up with a lawsuit.

My memory of the World War II wrecks that we dived on this momentous occasion left an unforgettable imprint on us all. We grasped more of an understanding as our skipper went over their history, and we realised just how many lives were lost. This has been so graphically portrayed in the recent spate of glory films such as 'Saving Private Ryan'. I can only imagine how frightening it must have been on those magnificent ships, for all those young men going off to do battle. It's pretty mind-boggling, especially when you see the Strathblayne, and the SS Ousso in Cherbourg, on our first dives of the week, before we set off to Normandy.

Normandy – Omaha Beach, the Empire Broadsword, the USS Susan B and the Anthony LST 527

There, we dived the Empire Broadsword and the USS Susan B, which I logged as being one of the best dives so far. The Anthony LST 527, listed as carrying twenty Sherman tanks, was absolutely fascinating, even though my torch went out after twenty minutes. Mike illuminated the way ahead with his torch, pointing out the tanks amongst all the corrosion and silt, as we swam over them. Sometimes, we'd pause for further inspection, or just to lighten the mood we'd climb inside some of the motor vehicles and make believe we were driving them.

But the best was yet to come; as we approached Omaha Beach, the skipper actually put on the video of 'Saving Private Ryan', to give more credibility to what we were about to see. I found this film very hard to watch at the cinema the first time round. It made me cry in uncontrollable sobs, as I buried my head in Mike's chest, trying not to acknowledge the sheer brutality of those soldiers being mown down by a constant barrage of bullets as they tried to disembark from their landing crafts. And as if that were not enough, if they did manage to avoid the bullets, most of them simply drowned from the bloody sheer weight of their kit bags and heavy rifles, like flies trapped in a honey pot. But I was assured that I was not the only one so affected, to judge from the flurry of hankies, the stunned silence that followed and the sheer reluctance to leave throughout the whole cinema.

HMS Sesame, the USS Meredith and the Sora

The strong currents didn't deter my enthusiasm in any way when we reached the wreck of the HMS Sesame, an ocean-going tug that towed the Mulberries into place, to help prevent any unsolicited landing craft. We found a shinbone on the USS Meredith III, so we looked for a nice place to bury it. It makes you shudder to think that someone died after being blown to bits whilst fighting for King and Country. The Sora was the last dive of the week. Mike got himself caught up in some mono-filament net, whilst digging about for something interesting. By the time I had cut him free he needed to be reminded to check his computer because we were already into decompression time. This meant that we would have to spend even longer on the shot line expelling the nitrogen build-up, to avoid the bends (we call this 'gassing off').

This was the longest dive of the week and one of the few times we finished with such a long decompression, as we believe it's good practice and makes for a safer dive to be on the shot line and 'gassing off' before your computer starts bleeping a warning. Sometimes, Mike has to take complete charge on the way up from a dive, because the particles in the water (a 'pea souper' we call it) are inclined to make me feel sick, especially when the current is running fast. To make sure you have expelled all the nitrogen from your body, you come up on the shot line in three stages. BSAC training requires a pause at nine metres, then a stop of three minute at six metres, and a further one minute to the surface. I have to close my eyes as it brings on a feeling not unlike vertigo, before being violently sick. It's just one of the many things I tend to put up with. It's not very nice, I know, but it doesn't put me off diving, as it is soon forgotten and I love my life as a rufty-tufty diver.

Some divers are sick underwater, straight into their demand valve (breathing apparatus), but I prefer to hold it all in until I reach the surface, because I think you then have less chance of inhaling it back and choking. But this has its drawbacks, as it gives me a thumping awful headache, as well as coming pretty close to unconsciousness. But I have complete faith in Mike as my dive buddy, and know I can rely on him to bring me safely to the surface, he's had to do so a couple of times, now. Besides, if anything happens to me, who's gonna cook the dinner?

We dived many more, similar wrecks that week. I have not mentioned them all, just the best of the bunch. It was a memorable dive time and one that I will never forget, not just for the sheer bravery of all those men who fought and died there, but also the senselessness of their loss of life. And although there is no comparison, I also suffered a personal loss of my own.

Deafness

After surfacing from the Strathblane, the first spectacular wreck of the week, I realised that the pressure had damaged my right ear. I was quite deaf, apart from a sound I could only describe as someone speaking through a broken megaphone. It took the entire week to get back to normal, although the symptoms would come back to haunt me ten years or so later.

I've come to the conclusion that, since there was no pain and no evidence of any blood from my ear at the time, the deafness must have been due to a slight inversion of the eardrum. I believe this is where the eardrum is stretched to a point just before perforation. The pressure on the eardrum is considerably worse in the first ten metres, which is where I stopped, than at a greater depth. Plus the bad visibility, and the fact that I had not yet had the chance to try out my new under suit, let alone dive any decent dives in my dry-suit for the past two years. So all these things combined probably left me feeling a little more apprehensive. In my opinion, this caused a slight panic attack on our first dive that week. After letting two of the other divers pass me on my way down the shot line during that dive, I stopped about halfway short of the bottom to give myself another five minutes or so to help calm me down, as the dive was quite a deep one. I thought I could see the seabed at one point from where I desperately clung, trying to convince myself not to give up and return to the surface in defeat. So after what seemed like an eternity I turned myself over and preceded headfirst down the remainder of the rope, ear clearing as I went. I descended further and further down into the darkness of the green, silty water, steadily pulling myself hand-over-hand, until I reached the anchor at the bottom of the shot line. I felt thoroughly pleased with myself for making the effort to overcome my fears, as the dive turned out to be a pretty good one after all.

I've always had a problem with my ears, right from my very first dive, and sometimes I suffer bad nosebleeds from the pressure. This is sometimes accompanied by spates of vertigo, especially when swimming up and over reefs too quickly. I tend to hold on to Mike, until it passes. But I have never let it put me off diving, even though I now have a real problem with my hearing and have to use a hearing aid.

Australia – Hong Kong

In 2002 we celebrated our 30th wedding anniversary with a month long holiday down under in Australia. The first four days of our tour were spent in Hong Kong, where we stayed in a luxury apartment-style room in Kowloon, just a bus ride to the ferry boat terminus for the journey over to Hong Kong Island. Further down the bay, two local boys boarded the ferry. They had a giant dragon costume over their heads, concealing most of their bodies except for their filthy feet that stuck out at the bottom. At first, we thought they must have been in a parade of some sort due to the dirty condition of the costume, until they started staggering and falling all over the place. As we looked on in disbelief they fell narrowly missing me into a heap on the floor. We could plainly see them through some rips in the material of the dragon's head. It was quite obvious that they were not drunk, but were in fact high on drugs, which they continued to smoke undercover of the costume. The conductor just turned a blind eye when he collected our tickets. It seemed that he had seen it all before, or maybe he didn't want any trouble.

As we approached Hong Kong Island I must admit that at first I was a little disappointed, as it was not what I had expected. I was under the illusion that it was more like Japan, with mandarin style houses with far-reaching views of mountainous regions, in a landscape of water gardens and carved wooden bridges under cherry blossom trees.

But as you approach the Island itself, the outline is just as spectacular as Manhattan in New York, with all the latest technology and laser-lighted buildings rising above the bay. Every conceivable gadget was displayed ready to purchase from a maze of shopping malls in intertwining corridors under the building, featuring magnificent sculptures and amazing waterfalls. And rising from the heart of the shopping centre there was a spectacular towering restaurant where you took a lift to the top and could view the city below, or eat in the revolving glass sided restaurant.

We also met an amazing couple who were well into their fifties. They told us about their travels around the world and about the times they spent staying in various different places in the Far East, like Laos, Cambodia and Vietnam, and other unusual places. They said they had no fear of the unknown and except for a few clothes in a rucksack; they lived solely on human kindness. It seemed very dangerous to me, especially when they told us of the time they got lost and ended up spending the night in the jungle in a cabin sleeping on just a cloth on a bamboo floor. We were so intrigued by their story that we missed our stop, and had to go back a couple of stops when the ferry turned around. By the time we got back I was feeling quite seasick. But I wouldn't have missed it for the world, and thought how brave they were, and how I envied them, even if it did seem a little bit dangerous.

Australia – Cairns and the Taka 2

We then travelled on to Queensland, then Sidney, then a four-day stopover in Bangkok on the way home. Ten of our days were divided between two destinations – five nights in Cairns, northeast of Queensland, and five on the Taka 2, a great livaboard boat with a great crew and a variety of different people from all walks of life. Some of the group were on their Gap Year from university; some were just on holiday but keen to dive the Great Barrier Reef, as we were.

The Taka 2 was sparsely furnished, but comfortable, and the food was quite good. We started our diving on some of the ribbon reefs in Challenger Bay, and then made our way further out into the Coral Sea where we dived some of the deeper reefs. We encountered some of the bigger pelagic, like enormous potato cod, which are so curious that they will come right up close and let you touch them. I did pose for a photo with puckered lips ready to kiss one very large one, but thought better of it when it came closer. Also, we had the very rare sighting of a ten- to twelve-foot shovel nosed ray. We were able to swim over it, getting close enough to take a very good picture, even though he was half-buried in the sand. He nonchalantly eyed us with one eye to see what the heck was disturbing his beauty sleep.

The shark feast at North Hole, Osprey was something else! It was one of the best dives ever, but getting there was horrendous. Everyone had been advised to take seasickness pills before bed, Mike included. He's never seasick as a rule, but he had to put his fingers down his throat to make himself sick, just to get through the night. That night the seawater gushed up over the sides of the boat with a vengeance. If you did manage to make it to the outside toilet in one piece without actually getting a soaking, you were probably less fortunate in the toilet, and got a cold shower whilst sitting there, as the water was coming clear over the six-foot doors. It was also very hard to read or even relax on your bunk, let alone sleep, as you were tossed around from side to side all night. A little after dawn we were woken and briefed on how to calmly sit and observe the dive guides at work throughout the shark feast. After a quick mug of coffee and an equipment check we were in the water, dropping down to about thirty-eight metres. We sat waiting at the bottom, on a rock formation aptly named The Amphitheatre for its uncanny resemblance to the theatre in Athens. The crew then lowered by rope a box of Chum, to encourage the sharks down to a point just above the flat, sandy bottom in front of us. This was followed by a long, spiked chain attached to a pulley, each spike impaling a tuna head. The sharks, lured initially by the smell of the Chum mixture of blood and guts, tore at the impaled tuna heads in a frenzy of bloody flesh gnashed between razor-sharp teeth. One of the crew even fed them and stroked them as they passed. We were totally rooted to the spot! It was terrifying, but enthralling at the same time. After the feeding, we were assured that if we were brave enough it would be all right to swim among the sharks that were left, as they had never before attacked anyone after the feeding frenzy. So of course we swam, all the time glancing over our shoulders whilst searching in the sand for shark's teeth. We managed to take some terrific pictures; one of my favourites is of several sharks swimming up behind me, as I look back in disbelief.

Most of the dive sights were very pretty, with lots of history, like Steve's Bonnie and Cod Hole. We took some beautiful pictures, but they lacked the colourful life of the Red Sea, due to El Niño (the warming of the sea) cutting short the growth, leaving a holocaust of dead, bony corral, with no fish life at all.

The Maureen of Dart

As a rule, on most boats, you are generally well looked after. An example was one of the trips out of Dartmouth we took in 2002, on a boat called the Maureen of Dart. She was like a home from home. We hired her for the week, to dive the Scilly Isles. Mike, our skipper, and Penny, his wife and our cook, were a team to be reckoned with, and knew just how to look after their customers. After each dive there was always a nice cup of steaming hot tea and a couple of biscuits waiting to warm you up. At dinner, the amount of food laid on was astonishing. Before we left harbour in Dartmouth, Penny would put an order in at the local bakery for half a dozen of the largest cakes and fruit pies. She served them with thick creamy custard, or a dollop of ice-cream, after a huge dinner every evening. She'd offer a choice of beef or lamb – both if you wanted – with as much potato as you could eat and a variety of vegetables, with a thick brown gravy. Sad to say, they are no longer a couple – perhaps they were too generous and couldn't make a profit on their livaboard.

The Edison and Wolf Rock Lighthouses, The Hathor, The Plympton, The Cita, The Maine and The Manacles

On the way out of the harbour we dived the rocks of the famous Edison Lighthouse. The whole of the rock face surrounding the Lighthouse was covered in beautiful jewel anemones, in every colour of the rainbow. Sometimes, I think I preferred the scenery here more than the diving. But I'm glad I didn't miss that one, or the Wolf Rock Lighthouse that is just as pretty. We dived some really good wrecks that week, like The Hathor and The Plympton that sunk one on top of the other. Whilst diving on another wreck, a boat called the Cita, we strayed onto another wreck, but we managed another try at the Cita at the end of the week. I wrote in my logbook that it was a nice wreck, but the visibility wasn't so good. The Maine was another good dive, where we saw a giant jellyfish. This freaked me out a bit because you need to be careful not to let their long tentacles come into contact with your skin at any time. I've seen what happened to one of our friends, Richard, when he came back from one of our dives in the Red Sea, covered in nasty, painful, red welts after he had tried to remove the jellyfish's long invisible tentacles from his face with his bare hands. The last dive of the week was a very pretty scenic one, called The Manacles. It had lots of fish life and large holes to poke around in, and was unexpectedly one of the best dives of the week.

Oban, Scotland – The SS Breda, The Tapti, The Hispania and The Port Napier

One of the best times, with a great sense of camaraderie that we still laugh about today, was on a trip we took in August 2003, on a livaboard up in Oban, Scotland, on a boat called the Kylebarn.

You could not have wished for better weather that week, with the whole of the country basking in extremely high temperatures, and the thermometers hitting the high seventies which I'm told is pretty good for that part of the country. The sea was like a millpond and the extremes of temperature between air and sea brought with it a soft blanket of mist. I thought it quite romantic standing on deck, staring out over a patchwork of mirrored calm each morning. Romantic as it was, it could also be a little eerie at times being totally shrouded in a cloak of mist, whilst waiting to be picked up after a hard dive. But to give him his due, the skipper, Jim, seemed to have no trouble in finding us.

Even though the visibility was pretty poor on the surface, underwater it was quite good, ten metres or more at times, making the many sunken wrecks scattered around the Islands far more accessible. We dived on The SS Breda, The Tapti and The Hispania just off The Isle of Mull, and The Port Napier off The Isle of Skye. Then on our return journey to Mull, we dived on The Aurania and The Thesis. All the wrecks were quite unique, with a variety of interests. The Tapti still had many recognisable features along her entire length, with masses of encrusted colourful sea-life and a separated, but equally impressive, bow section rising nearly fifteen metres from the seabed. The 402 foot three-decked Breda, a 6941 tonne, flat-bottomed steel steamer included its rudder. Towards the stern, the cabins can be explored up to two levels above deck. The chassis of a lorry still had a couple of tyres visible, and was encrusted with sea feathers. The hull, too, was covered with sea feathers as well as 'dead-man's fingers' and coloured anemones. And perhaps the best of the bunch – The Hispania, with her story of her brave Captain who refused to leave and went down with his ship. The funnel protrudes up to twelve metres from the wreck, and it also has great swim troughs to her bridge and cabins, making it seem like she's still afloat. The Aurania is a mass of tangled wreckage, strewn over a large area, with her massive boilers still sitting six to seven metres proud of the seabed. They provide a home to huge shoals of different fish, including angelfish and huge conger eels, octopus and crabs.

The Kylebarn, Jim and Sandy

The Kylebarn, our home for the week, was a converted fishing boat that had a regular coating of tar that probably helped keep her watertight for her fishing days. But it didn't work quite so well for a dive boat. The remnants of tar got onto everything that touched her deck, so you dared not put your bags down, even to kit up. Every morning there was a bit of a sprint as we clambered for the best places to put our kitbags, like the flat top of the wooden net and rope housing under the windows of the wheelhouse. But that was nothing compared to what Jim, our tight-fisted, mean-minded skipper had in store. Well, the Scots are perceived as being 'careful' in general, but he quite literally took the biscuit.

For instance – you didn't dare leave your wetsuit out to dry overnight, because, if Jim was in a hurry to leave harbour next morning, he didn't give a toss if anyone's gear was hanging over the side to dry. Mike found this out to his cost, when the air vent on his sleeve was totally mangled as Jim manoeuvred his way around a boat that had tied on to us the previous evening. When questioned later, his response was,
"You don't expect me to clear stuff left hanging about before we leave each morning, do you?"

"No," said Mike in a bitter voice, "but a warning the night before might have been nice!"
As we stood around in our gear, waiting to be let off the boat for our dive the next day, Johnny Watts made a comment on the time Jim took, and said that he should know better than keeping us hanging around, as if we were much longer we were likely to miss our window for slack tide. Unbeknown to John, it was within earshot of Jim, who had been sitting resting his arm out of the open window of the wheelhouse. Jim angrily replied from above, saying in a broad Scottish accent,

"I've met your type before and I daresay I will meet them again!"
Well, this was very hard for John to live down, even though he did offer an apology at the time. He was very embarrassed every time it was mentioned, and he always made sure of Jim's whereabouts after that. After our dive Jim would make a cup of tea. I'm not exaggerating when I say that he put only one teabag into a large pot, for all twelve of us. And we were only allowed one custard cream each! If anyone dared complain, he would say in his broad Scottish accent,
"I did put out thirteen."
The meals were a bit of a fiasco, too, with Jim constantly complaining that we were greedy and ate too much.

After a long crossing, we moored up for the night in a place called Tobermory, on The Isle of Mull. That evening, we made our way to the rowdiest pub, boasting a host of entertainment. I took some stick from the boys when I got chatting to a pretty woman who lived a couple of doors away, when she invited me over for a visit before we left. Shame we never made time to go. I certainly could have done with some female company before the off, especially after being trapped for a week on a boat full of men. They don't realise just how boring it can be with all that male testosterone flying about.

Next morning, we decided it would be a good time to do a spot of shopping and sight-seeing in Tobermory, whilst Jim refuelled and got the last of his provisions. Beds of plants, in striking nautical themes, had been cut into the grass verges that led down to a haven of pastel painted houses, with quaint little shops and restaurants dotted in-between. Some of the shops had leaded, stained-glass windows, depicting colourful sailing boats and all things nautical. An abundance of decorative flowering plants in strikingly beautiful colours brimmed over wooden troughs lined the length of the quay and every lamp-post had its flower display trailing from enormous hanging baskets, strung together with an array of colourful bunting, blowing fiercely in readiness for the forthcoming regatta weekend.

Johnny Watts treated us all to a mid-morning scone when we returned. He thought it would be nice to eat them before our mid-morning dive, prior to lunch. This is standard practice on most dive boats, dive and then your meal, because you are usually quite ravenous after diving and it also gives you enough time to rest and digest before your teatime dive which is usually before dinner. The exception is in the case of a night dive, when dinner is usually held over until after the dive, with tea, cakes and biscuits in between to tide you over – if you have a good host! Anyway, Sandy the cook-come-cabin boy was genuinely dismayed at our request for some butter. He said he would have to sneak it out of the kitchen because Jim would certainly not have approved of us using up our meagre quota before the end of the week. Jim was also disapproving later that day, questioning Sandy as to why lunch was not served at its 'usual time', and demanding that in future we ate lunch at mid-morning, half an hour or so before our dive. This didn't really give us time to digest it, but it would mean that he could then serve dinner as early as he could get away with. He could then get moored up and all could go for a leisurely pint down the pub before dark, he said. But the skipper of the boat moored next to us on the day of our arrival, had already informed us before we boarded that this was so as to give enough time for us to charge our torches at the pub before closing time. When we questioned Jim later, he totally denied it, with the plausible explanation that he was frightened we would over-load the generator, if we all plugged in at the same time. But we think it was more to do with getting us all off the boat whilst it was still light, thus saving the running cost of the generator.

We also visited one of the local pubs, on one of the more remote Islands, where we were perceived as being a religious group by the locals. I think it was because, compared to them, we all looked so clean and smart. Some of the women were very

scruffy, with unkempt hair and long dirty fingernails, like witches. Their clothes were as bad as their hair. I'm sure I saw a couple of broomsticks tucked away behind the bar on our way out. The men-folk looked equally as bad, if not worse, some having long, dirty grey beards down to their waists. I noticed that they seemed fascinated by my feet, and kept staring at them whenever they thought I wasn't looking. For a while, I wondered what they were looking at. Then someone mentioned that they were fascinated by my toenails. By the look of some of the women I don't think any of them had ever worn nail polish, let alone seen someone with a French manicure, especially on the toenails, which was the trend then. On our way out of the pub that evening, a kind woman pressed a plastic bag into Andy's hand saying,
"You will need this."
He thanked her for it, but didn't have a clue what it was for, until we got a little way up the road. Then we discovered that it was to put over his head, before we were totally engulfed in midges. Luckily for me, I had a hood on my white sweatshirt, which was totally covered by the time we got back.

Sandy

We'd usually have a glass or two of wine with dinner and toddy or two of alcohol before bed. We brought the alcohol on board at the start of the week. Andy made a point of marking his brandy bottle with a line, to make sure no-one helped themselves, after he had gone to bed. All the bottles seemed a little short most morning, and Sandy seemed a little worse for wear on more than one occasion.

One morning, we realised that he'd definitely been drinking heavily the previous night when he lay down on a towel in the middle of the deck, using his rucksack as a pillow, getting in everyone's way throughout the day. He totally ignored Jim's constant requests for help with manning the boat, and said that he would stay put until he was paid the money he thought he was due. He told us that he needed to buy himself some shorts, as his new jeans were getting ruined by all the cooking and upkeep of the boat. When Jim tried to get him to move, it was quite obvious that he was paralytic. I don't think Sandy would have stood up to Jim without his alcoholic courage. As he had said he had no money, we concluded that he had been consuming then watering down our alcohol whilst we were all asleep. He had asked us all quite discreetly the day before, for the loan of some money. But as we hadn't known him that long, I'm ashamed to say that we all declined. However, we found out later that Jim gave him a ten-pound sub most nights, before they went to the pub, to keep him quiet. But he then demanded that Sandy pay for his drinks as well as his own. On finding this out we had a tenner a head whip-round for him at the end of the week. We heard later after we left that Jim had realised the error of his ways and offered Sandy a pay rise, with a regular payday to keep him on.

I wrote this little ditty in the Captain's Comment book before we left:

'Sandy would be handy, if he keeps his mitts off Andy's
'brandy!'
But some smart Alek's comment, said it all, really, it read:
'Its life, Jim, but not as we know it'!

Tanzania

In September 2007, I won an all-inclusive diving holiday for two to Tanzania. I nearly rejected my prize as I had difficulty understanding what was being said on the telephone. The man speaking to me had a very thick Italian accent, and after repeating; "Pardon, can you speak a little slower, please" several times, to no avail, I rejected the holiday, and put the phone down, mindful of stories of time-share scams and fraud.

But a little thought entered my head – we had filled in several holiday competition forms at the International Dive Show that year. So I decided to check if the phone number was stored in the telephone call-back, and as luck would have it, it was – it was a genuine phone-call. Can you imagine the shock and horror I felt as I realised that I had turned down the holiday of a lifetime! And when the chap answered, Mike tried to explain and apologise for my actions. He was not amused! But Mike assured him it was a genuine mistake, that I am a little hard of hearing and have great difficulties with foreign accents over the phone. The man assured Mike that the call was not a hoax, and said that he would contact us with more information the next day. I think I am a lucky person generally, but have never won anything of any great worth – but this holiday was worth in excess of two and a half thousand pounds. It was based in a stunning location on the African coast, called Mafia Island, Tanzania.

At first we thought the whole venture a bit daunting – especially with a name like Mafia Island. We wondered if we might be in danger of being mugged, or kidnapped, or worse. Then there was the amount of preparation beforehand – it was enough to put a sane person off the whole idea. Firstly, you had to take anti-malaria tablets for weeks before and after the trip; then you had to top up your polio and hepatitis injections, as well as having yellow fever jabs at fifty pounds a time. Plus we had to get extra health insurance. All in all, we spent four hundred pounds or so before we even got out of the country. But I am pleased to say that nothing untoward happened, the place was absolutely magic, and in fact it was probably one of the most chilled dive holidays we've ever experienced.

As soon as the plane set down in Tanzania's Dar Es Salaam airport we were treated like VIPs. As we awaited the plane for Mafia Island, we were taken to a smart hotel along the beach. After a nap and a shower, we had lunch and chilled over a cool drink on the jetty of a local restaurant with stunning views of the tropical paradise we were heading for. Eventually, a small plane arrived, with only a dozen seats or so. At five-foot-ten-inches tall, and with a rucksack on my back, I had some difficulty in boarding.

Arriving on the Island, we were greeted by a man driving a safari jeep. After checking our paperwork (and charging an entrance fee) we were on our way, perched high atop the jeep, towards our destination. Mafia Lodge was accessed only by a couple of miles of arid dirt track, lined with palm trees. On the drive, we passed through a typical African village. It had a small community hall at the centre, where chickens and goats ran freely around the square. The village women were dressed from head to toe in their traditional dress, their shapely bodies swathed in tightly-wrapped brightly coloured material, and their hair wrapped tightly in similarly bright turban head wraps. Some were chatting inside the doorways of their tiny shacks, whilst others were brushing the dirt away from outside their ramshackle homes with what looked like witches' brooms, made from a few twigs attached to a stick. The men-folk were a lot taller than the women, strong looking, and many dressed in a similar fashion. Others favoured a more westernised dress, with peaked caps, jeans, tee-shirts and white trainers. They congregated in the main town on the outskirts of the village around an assortment of make-shift shops – rusty corrugated tin roofs balancing on crumbling walls, seemingly held together with layers of torn, washed-out posters. Some shopkeepers sold their goods from the huts, sheltered from the intense heat of the sun, whilst others sold from their bicycles on the kerbside. Each day they rode along the dirt track, hanging bags of home-produce on the handlebars, or balancing stacks of fresh eggs on either side of the saddle, thirty or forty boxes at a time. Others walked to the shops balancing their goods on their heads with only their turbans to give some protection from the weight of their burdens.

Yet for all our interest in them, and the benefits of the extra work we brought to the area, it was an uncomfortable feeling to see their dislike of this intrusion of westerners, the overt display of inequality and a wealth they could only dream about. You could see the resentment in their eyes as we passed by, sat up high in a big safari jeep, with digital cameras. Gold jewellery, bulging cases and rucksacks splashed all over with designer labels and dressed to the nines in designer gear like some sort of VIP.

Mafia Lodge

We stayed with a handful of other guests at the Mafia Lodge, a huge thatched beachside hut. In the stunning tropical gardens, the native humming-birds busily swooped from one exotic flower to another. Their flight feathers fanned you as you walked the length of the path leading down to the gleaming white sands of the beach, lapped by an azure blue sea. The dive centre was perched at its edge, under a canopy of giant palm trees, bent low with coconuts.

One afternoon the electricity was playing up throughout the lodge. That afternoon, we decided to have tea on the veranda to take in the beautiful sea views. Mike offered to make the tea using the little electric element we had taken away with us. We sat and watched the sun go down as we drunk our tea. Mike mentioned that the electricity had failed just as the water had boiled, and he had hung the element over the plug box to cool down.
"I hope you remembered to switch the element off before you hung it up," I said.

With that, Mike leapt up and we both ran back inside to find the room was filled with smoke. Flames were literally licking the ceiling of the thatched roof and the plug box had already melted. In a panic and a flurry of teacloths and whatever else we could lay our hands on, we managed to beat out the flames, leaving a terrible black streak up the wall and a layer of black ash covering the entire room, the bed and all the furniture. We went to confess the unfortunate incident to the receptionist, but before we could explain properly, the electricity went off again. The receptionist told us that the supply had been going off and on all day, playing havoc with her computer, and with the power surges she was not surprised the plug box had caught fire. Within minutes, we had an army of staff apologizing profusely, and helping us to move to a new room. We couldn't believe our luck!

Because it was the end of season we were the only people on the dive boat. Mario, our Italian dive guide and owner of the dive school, said that he had never before felt so 'laid back' on a dive, because we were such accomplished divers. We took it as a great compliment that he felt he could just chill out and enjoy his time with us.

Mafia Island

On one dive, we went out beyond the Bay of Mafia Island, hoping to glimpse some of the many whales that pass by. Mario would only take experienced divers, as the current was very strong, and it was late in the season and visibility was poor. The majority of the whales had already left for the open seas of the Indian Ocean, even though we could not see them, we were fortunate enough to encounter a few, and hear them 'singing'. I will never forget the experience as wave after wave of sweet, high-pitched 'awwoohhoo' washed over us as they called to each other, in the murky blue of the channel – it made me tingle from head to toe as the vibrations went right through me.

As a treat, Mario introduced us to some of his none-diving friends who were visiting him, and we all went to a little isolated, uninhabited Island, out in the deep blue sea of the Indian Ocean. The woman amongst our party was not well on the boat trip, and sat with her head on her knees for the whole of the journey. Talk about unprepared! Although she had admitted that she occasionally suffered from seasickness, she thought that the sea was very calm and that she would be all right for the two-hour journey without any seasickness medication. I offered her some of the ginger I always take with me as a precaution, but I don't think she understood its usefulness in easing seasickness, as she said she felt too sick to take it! I know how she felt, as I always suffer from seasickness and will never undertake a boat trip without first taking anti-seasickness medication.

On the journey out, we saw a boat so laden down that it appeared only a couple of inches from capsizing. The passengers were carrying great big parcels of food, barrels of fresh water and some livestock, across to the other Island. Another boat, apparently full of working men, came frighteningly close to ours, which was very unnerving as there were stories of people being kidnapped in underdeveloped countries. We must have appeared pretty wealthy to them, dressed in our designer garb, with a great big boat all to ourselves.

After about two hours, we reached our destination, and anchored up for our dive. After diving, we strolled over to where the other couple were now sheltering under a makeshift sunshade. They told us that there had been a heavy downpour whilst we were diving. It didn't seem too bad to us, and besides we were still in our wet suits and by then the sun was shining through white fluffy clouds. We sat down to eat the very nice lunch kindly provided by Mario. After a little nap, we decided to take a stroll around the Island, which was probably the length of a couple of football pitches, and half as wide. We examined the many crustaceans that scurried about the spectacular white sands seeking shelter from the intense heat, many decked out with fronds of weed and flora waving from their shells. We counted the many colours of several types of starfish that had also been caught up by the waves, which were now breaking hard and fast all around us. And so we were forced to leave our beautiful Island with all its treasures, before it became engulfed in its blue watery grave once again.

Our dive guide, William, a native of these parts, invited us to explore an inhabited Island the next day. We watched from the comfort of our boat as large bundles of goods and water were delivered to the Island, from a boat similar to the one we had passed yesterday. After landing, we all trekked down a well-worn path through the lush undergrowth, to a clearing at the heart of the Island. We saw some men chopping down trees, and further along we saw them working on a boat. They looked at us with some suspicion in their eyes and waved us away when we held up the cameras to take pictures. I was lucky and managed to get a photograph of the boat they were working on, as well as a good picture of the indigenous pre-historic Boabab Tree, pronounced BEY-oh-Bab also known as the Monkey Bread Tree which can grow between 16- 82ft in height, with a trunk girth of 10-14meters or more. They bear a heavy white flower 12cm across, that are primarily pollenated by the fruit bat, this produce's an egg shaped fruit that's extremely nutritious.

Another extraordinary sight was the hundreds of giant fruit bats hanging from the canopy in the clearing high above us. They were totally cocooned from the heat by their very large wings, but were obviously disturbed by our presence as they flew erratically from branch to branch, screeching discordantly.

The indigenous people live a simple life, in huts made and thatched from leaves, woven in a basket-like fashion from the palm trees that grew in abundance all over the Island. Each house seemed to have its own little henhouse, resting on stilts, made from layers of dried leaves and thatched in the same fashion as the houses. We counted several mother hens, closely followed by their flocks of little fluffy chicks, scratching for worms and bugs in the undergrowth.

VIPs at the Hospital on Mafia Island

The Island was also a place of learning, with a community school right at its heart alongside a welfare centre/hospital for all the inhabitants in the local area. It was certainly an eye-opener when we were shown around the junior girls' classroom, as visiting VIPs. The girls looked very smart in their school uniforms of little green dresses with yellow collars. They seemed delighted to be able to practise their English on us, and we joined them in the old nursery song: 'heads, shoulders knees and toes…'! To their delight we then played back the film of them, which we had taken on our digital cameras. The classroom itself consisted of a dirt floor in a wire enclosure, rather like a large chicken coop. In the African climate it made good sense as it allowed the air to circulate. It was sparsely furnished with small wooden desks and stools for the children to sit on, clustered together in small groups. A large blackboard with chalks and an old-fashioned felt rubber stretched the length of the 'wall', behind a large desk and chair for the teacher. In the corner, a door led to the main part of the school and to the senior classrooms. We could not see around it, but I think it was of a much sturdier construction.

We also visited the clinic that also doubled as the hospital. The only one of its kind, it also served many of the surrounding Islands. The Head Nurse informed us that it took about fifteen minutes to process a blood sample, and appeared quite shocked when she learned that in such an affluent country as ours it could take up to a fortnight or longer. They seemed very pleased when we gave them a donation, and offered us a seat and a cool drink before we made our way back through the lush undergrowth. On the trip back, we took the opportunity to get to know William a little better. He told us more of the history of the Island and more about himself. As a boy, he almost lost one of his big toes due to a worm infestation. He was educated on the main land at Tanzania, where English was learned as a second language, and was lucky enough to meet Mario, who was looking for cheap labour. As he showed a keen interest in diving, Mario gave him the opportunity to learn and qualify as a Dive guide, with a steady income.

The Red Sea, Egypt

I've lost count of the number of times we, the Havering & Ilford 49ers, have dived in the Red Sea in Egypt. Just four-and-a-half hours flight from the UK, and situated on the southern tip of the Sinai Peninsula, six bays make up the resort of the divers' Mecca – Sharm El Sheikh. About twenty minutes' drive away from the more exclusive and quieter Sharks Bay and White Knight's Bay, lays my favourite, the livelier main tourist district of Naama Bay. The region has few cloudy days, and only 2.5mm of rain per year, with a temperature that can reach a sweltering 40+ degrees centigrade in summer, falling to around 19 degrees in winter. You can count on good visibility all year round, making it a very favourable dive destination.

Twice yearly for the past fifteen years, my husband Mike, our Club's Membership Secretary and Bar Steward, has booked the best deals on the web, catering for the many diving levels of our club members and accommodation for their friends and families.

I have collected some amazing stories over the years whilst staying in Egypt, and a few more whilst staying on our favourite livaboard vessel, a converted Russian minesweeper, The Sea Queen. She had been completely refurbished with all mod cons to cater for parties of about twenty-four, plus a couple of dive guides and a crew of nine.

Each morning, we gathered on the jetty for a day-trip to Ras Mohammed National Park, from the throng that greeted us in the hustle and bustle of Naama Bay. We boarded the day boat, which had been packed to the gills (pardon the pun!) with dozens of bottles of 'pop', earthy tasting spring water and enough food for a full-blown lunch. Trolley loads of diving gear and air cylinders trundled up and down the diesel-stained, weathered pontoon. A maze of guy-ropes snaked around the ankles of the many passengers waiting patiently to board their allocated day-boat, hopeful to be among the first to leave the fume filled heat haze now rising above the jetty. The constant honking of horns echoed above the sound of revving engines set on standby to do battle at a moment's notice, ready to reverse into the smallest available space in this divers' sea fairing circus.

We were greeted by our crew as we stepped onto a plank walkway which leads to the equipment deck behind the ladders at the stern of the boat, which also housed its own air compressor. Air cylinders rested in their dock-holes around its perimeter, behind a seat wide enough to house an equipment box, i.e. an old crate underneath and overhead a line of hangers awaited our wetsuits. The dining room doors were also located on this deck, right in front of the large hatch concealing the stairwell down to the engine room deep in the boat's fume-filled bowels.

The dining room was clad floor to ceiling with highly polished wood with an inlaid jacquard pattern. Window seats fitted with long, padded cushions lined the walls behind several tables surrounded with chairs in a similar polished wood. Over a wood-clad counter top a niche held a tap, connected on the other side of the wall to the constantly boiling samovar. A shelf held a variety of different teas and coffees, solely for our use at our leisure. A Moorish influenced mirrored door concealed the hatch to the kitchen. Out through the double exit doors of the dining room several stairs led down to an inner glass door leading to the carpeted corridor of which were our bunkrooms and various sleeping arrangements. The restful décor of this cosy little corridor was how I should think it might look on a small cruise-ship. All the rooms were well-equipped with en-suite showers and toilets, and with independent air conditioning.

Some passengers preferred to sleep on the sundeck under the stars, on the soft, comfortable sun-lounger mattresses, which were provided with enough space for everyone to chill-out and sunbathe after a good day's diving. The downside is the constant interruptions from the crew, who also like to sleep on the sundeck, especially if it was particularly warm. However, I preferred to sleep on my little bunk, as I needed as much peace and quiet as I could get whilst trying to sleep in those cramped and sometimes claustrophobic conditions.

Another comfortable place to sleep was the sumptuous fully airconditioned lounge below. It was a nice, cool place to chill if it was very hot, and you could watch TV or a film on the DVD box. Unfortunately, this area also had its disadvantages, as the exit was extensively used by the crew as it led through to the ship's bow and the wheel-house. It was also the place where the ship's captain and some of the crew slept. Back out through the lounge, the hall and wide landing had been fitted with toilet and shower facilities for the crew. The very low, arch-shaped doorway had a cushion nailed to it, to render it less painful if you forgot to duck. It could be even more painful if you had your glasses perched on top of your head, as I found out several times the hard way. In fact, we all managed to bash our heads, especially after a few bevvies. The arched doorway led out on to an open-sided deck, where we would gather to chill in the cross breezes, with a beer or glass of wine after dinner. A water cooler stood just outside the door, next to a cluster of a dozen or so comfortable bucket seat wicker chairs with matching glass-topped coffee tables. Music played in the background from a music system behind the bar over-looking another cluster of tables and chairs set around a small dance airier, with a shiny steel pole to support the ceiling in the centre of the floor. Against the wall opposite, stacked up beside a fully-stocked 'fridge containing 'pop', provided by the proprietor of the boat, there were half-a-dozen or so crates of 'Sakara' – our contribution of the local beer, bought at the wholesalers before boarding for our week's diving.

This part of the boat, the middle deck, housed the rib with its tender and a winch for ease of storage. It was also the place that the crew liked to gather in the evening, smoking cigarettes or a little weed and played cards, or they just dozed under the boats, because even after a hard day's work, they could still be called upon throughout the evening. Besides cards one of their favourite games was Django or Towers and they liked to play in teams that included us where possible. It was customary, if your team lost the game, to do the 'honourable thing' and jump overboard; I think I could be forgiven for sometimes believing it was more a game of 'chicken' between them and us.

One night, after losing our game, one of our guys refused point-blank to jump overboard. So I stood up, in my chiffon summer dress, and to everyone's astonishment, climbed the side-rail and calmly jumped overboard. So as not to be outdone by a mere woman, he finally relented, saying as he jumped in that he was going to jump in anyway. Secretly, I thought, 'Oh yeah – sure!' It was not as bad as you might think though, as the boat was fully illuminated underneath, and you would be unlucky to see anything much bigger than a parrot fish that close to the reef.

One evening, after a couple of games, I noticed that the captain had changed his shorts for a traditional wrap-round skirt. I didn't give it another thought, other than he might be a little warm, until his team suddenly lost. He jumped up onto the side rail, lifted his skirt and did a 'moony' before jumping overboard. This was a man who hardly spoke a word of English, but gaily entered into the spirit of things – as you might imagine, we all thought it extremely funny, and nearly fell out of our chairs with laughter.

They all seemed to be very good sports, though, and liked nothing better than to get us to join them, especially when they entertained us with their traditional dance. Mike, being a bit of a comedian himself, liked to take things a step further and dress the prat – sorry- part! With a little help from me, lashings of red lipstick and my bikini top stuffed with socks to enhance the shape of his boobs, a silky wrap tied around his bottom and a pair of high heels to accentuate his shapely legs, I can honestly say he looked as good as any Drag Queen – a real Belly Dancer – and I mean 'belly'! One night, after saying that he was not going to dress up ever again, he disappeared on his own. Half an hour later re re-appeared in much the same costume with a sheer wraparound and obligatory high heels. The difference this time was that he had managed to squeeze his head into an old, black, wet-look diving hood, worn backwards but with slits cut into it for his eyes and mouth. He looked the epitome of an exotic dancer, and at one point he even hooked his leg around the pole in the middle of the dance floor, shaking his behind and poking out his tongue in a most suggestive manner. As soon as we saw him, everyone roared with laughter, we laughed until it hurt and we couldn't laugh any more. Some of the guys were rolling around on the floor, crying with laughter at his antics – even the crew who are generally a little reserved were falling about laughing. It felt so good to see the crew laughing and joining in the fun. These guys come from some of the poorest parts of the world, and don't seem to have a lot of anything, in some cases not even a change of clothes. It's probably more important to them to own a mobile phone to keep in touch with the family than to own a full change of clothing – something we take very much for granted these days. So you can imagine how very disappointed they were when Mike refused to do it again the following year, saying it was all becoming a little bit predictable. All the divers and crew said how much they looked forward to his spectacular performances, as did I.

I can't imagine what it must be like to have to work two or three months on the trot, with only a hand-out of our tips to look forward to at the end of the week. The tips were given to the Captain, and he shared them among the crew as he saw fit. I've never liked this arrangement, and voiced my opinion many times to no avail. The youngest crew member always seems to end up with just a pittance, leaving him with very little for any sort of entertainment, or for the little luxuries we take for granted such as deodorant or toothpaste.

So I always took some little treats with me – cigarettes, sweets and gum, and chocolate. One time I also took the game of Towers with me, which pleased them all very much as their last one went missing when the boat was in dry dock for refurbishment.

When we got home after that holiday one of the guys gave Mike a proper Egyptian yashmak that seemed to revive his interest a little. The following year he went all out to please us. He wore his new yashmak over a really ugly mask 'face', a long black wig with cerise streaks, false boobs under his bikini top, and a black, wrap-around skirt covered in long silver beads that jangled and glittered when he moved. He only removed the yashmak, revealing his ugly mask, at the very end of his dance, frightening us all into hysterical laughter again. It remains to be seen whether we'll have a repeat performance this year – which will take some beating! The fun and camaraderie was another aspect of livaboard diving that we very much look forward to, especially as we aren't getting any younger.

The Thistlegorm

Another advantage of livaboard diving in the Red Sea is that you have free, unlimited access to the bigger wrecks, like the wreck of The Thistlegorm that lies in the Straits of Gubal, in the Northern Red Sea. She was a cargo ship carrying munitions and assorted vehicles including Norton and BSA motorbikes, as well as rifles and wellington boots. She was targeted by two Heinkel F111's and sunk in 1941. It must be one of the most interesting of the larger wrecks, it's probably one of the biggest, and certainly one of the most spectacular we have been fortunate enough to dive. There is so much to see that it is impossible to cover it all on a single tank of air, and no matter how often you dive it, you will always find something of interest.

About fifteen years ago, when we first dived on it, part of a consignment of motorcycles (like the one Steve McQueen rides in The Great Escape) still had their leather seats intact! Plus we could see rows of army trucks, and we could climb in and out of the steam locomotives, which still seemed in good condition. Wellington boots were also scattered all over the deck. Over the years, after several visits, we were amazed to discover the extent of erosion, as well as astonished at the lengths divers will go to for a trophy (albeit a stolen one). After years of being over-dived, the trapped air-bubbles have caused serious erosion and the ship has become structurally unsound, with some parts near to collapse. The local authorities have great concerns about the wreck being so intensively dived, and there were rumours that at one point they were considering closing the dive site down altogether.

The most spectacular part of The Thistlegorm wreck, for me, is where it has been blown wide apart, just as if it had been sliced down the middle with a giant breadknife, and has fallen open into two separate halves. As you swim from one part to the other, looking down from the top of its broken back, the view is incredible. With good visibility you can look right through her damaged sections, and you get a real sense of the size of the ship, and the extent of the damage is laid bare. Sometimes, the visibility is a little murky, like a foggy day. The current can be quite treacherous at this point, and you could quite easily be swept up and away. When it is running fast, you have to get right down between the two halves when swimming across but it is still well worth the swim as there is another train engine lying in the sand alongside her, and it is well worth exploring. Plus you need to be good on air as it is a place where you can easily run out, especially as some people tend to chuff it (breathe heavily). It is a long swim and quite an effort against an on-coming current, especially if you are older or not quite fit enough. It's also easy to get lost inside the massive structure, and you must stick to the planned route. As BSAC members, our motto is: 'Plan the dive, and dive the plan'. This makes for less confusion when under water. I totally rely on Mike to lead the way as he has a great sense of direction (both in and out of the water) and seems to take in everything that is relevant for our safe return. I suppose you could say that being a Black Cabbie certainly has its advantages here. It is said that 'doing the Knowledge' helps produce a plumper hippocampus the part of the brain primarily associated with navigation skills, learning, organization and memory. You do sometimes get the reckless diver who doesn't stick to the plan and consequently has to cut their dive time short for some reason or other, and even occasionally one who does the unthinkable and comes up without their dive buddy. But on the whole I'm glad to say that this rarely happens with our club members.

A drawback of this dive is its popularity, with so many divers kicking up the silt throughout the day; you need to be up very early in the morning to get a good, clear dive. If you are in the vicinity, this means about five o'clock in the morning, but even earlier if you are coming from one of the harbours.

Also, as I remember from my first dives, there can be a large amount of shot-line being carelessly dropped over the side by unscrupulous boat handlers all hustling to get their divers into the water before the rush. Of late, there are new regulations as to where to drop anchor, which I understand is now limited to specific points to make it safer, and to protect the precious coral reefs.

Shark Reef and the Yolanda

One of my favourite reefs in Ras Mohammed which has to be seen to be believed is called Shark and Yolanda reef, where sometimes the current can be pretty strong, making it virtually inaccessible, and at other times as gentle as a pussy-cat. If you approach it via the wall, passing the old Observatory (I believe it was used to count how many sharks that passed this point, hence its name), it is absolutely breath taking encrusted with flora, and teaming with life. Rounding the wall, reminds me of the Abyss from the film of the same name as it drops off to around about eight hundred metres, and can be very daunting for the novice diver. I have seen some of the toughest divers clinging to the walls with their eyes on stalks. But I just love the feeling of flying, with an eagle's-eye view into infinity, whilst looking out for the bigger pelagic fish (fish that live neither at the bottom nor at the top of the body of water) and hopefully a glimpse of a shark or two into the bargain. As you near the end of the wall, the swim in-between is called the saddle, and it is bathed in a warm, welcoming sunny current. It has some of the prettiest gardens, with an abundance of all sorts of corals and colourful fish life.

Further up the reef just past the saddle, as you round the bend it spreads out like a giant skirt as you swim around its curves at the bottom. You can swim on and on at the very edge where you might be lucky to spot a shark of two out in the blue, before you feel the pull of the strong current outside the reef. You are swept along on the return journey over some of the most heavily laden coral gardens that completely cover this most attractive area. At the bottom of the slope presumably to create a buffer as I usually suffer a sudden surge of vertigo, I usually swim with my eyes closed, holding on to Mike's hand, as the current sweeps me up and over the shelving to the highest reaches of the reef. The wreck of the Yolanda – which sunk in 1987 after hitting the reef – stands tall at the top like the bare bones left over from a rack of lamb after the feast, her cargo of sanitary ware and jumble of white toilets littered around her. If you look a little closer, you may also see the remnants of the Captain's car, distinguishable by its tyres still visible on its wheels, sticking out from the wreckage. But for me, one of the best parts of the whole dive-site is where we prepare to finish the dive at about 15 metres or so, near the top of the reef. As we 'gas-off' before our final ascent, from this vantage point, with good visibility, we get a bird's-eye view of the whole structure of the wreck beneath and the finer details, in stunning technicolour, of all the fascinating fish life that live in and frequent this spectacular reef.

The Elphinstone Reef

The Elphinstone Reef in the Southern Red Sea of Marsa Alam, Egypt, is one of those dive sites you would not want to miss! It is well-known for its very strong currents that split around its elongated-shape forcing the water into different directions, creating a vortex with a dishwasher effect in-between. The day we dived there to see the hammerhead sharks, the current was extremely strong. We were briefed to dive from the flatter side of the reef, swimming out against the strong current, away from the flatter side. This was normal practice as, I presume, the reef helped create a buffer as we entered open water, essentially helping to prevent us from being swept out. But there were so many divers in the water already, and our dive guide didn't want to abandon the dive totally, that he changed his brief at the last moment. So now we were swimming with the current away from the jagged end, with not much protection to buffer us from behind, not good practice. But you assume that the dive guides know best, and it did make swimming down to forty-seven metres out in the blue fairly easy. Yet after ascending up to the shallower depth of twenty metres as briefed, the situation was made far worse. Try as we might to swim back, the current, which was splitting in different directions, made it virtually impossible. And what made it seem worse at the time; we could clearly see how easy it was for the divers swimming to the plateau at forty metres. But against the vortex of water on this side of the reef, we stood little chance.

After what seemed like forever, with my chest heaving as though I had just run a marathon, a quick glance at my computer told me that I was well into decompression – not a good place to be whilst still swimming for your life. I pointed this out to my all-time dive buddy (Mike) a couple of times, and when he finally understood my message his response was so quick that he nearly broke my wrist as he twisted it for a second glance at my computer. I also gave him the signal that I was extremely tired and out of breath. He immediately suggested we swim out wide of the reef, away and out of the pull of the currents, bringing us gently back to the side of the reef - which we all did. (It's Mike's quick and decisive thinking that makes him such an excellent Dive Leader.) I then signalled that we should 'gas-off' (decompress) as near to the top of the reef as was safe, and for as long as possible to rid our bodies of any residual gases. Mike quickly made a few signals to one of the other buddy couples in our group, indicating what our intentions were, and we slowly set off on our own, to the more comfortable level of about eight metres. We swam over the top of the reef and to our astonishment found ourselves looking down into a giant crater, a great haven for all sorts of sea-life, sheltering in its comfortable, warm hollow, away from the hostile current that rushed around it. We gingerly swam over a giant moray eel stretched out, taking in the warm rays of the sun. He eyed us menacingly, with a look that seemed to ask how we dare disturb his beauty sleep. Several giant groupers seemed equally surprised by our presence.

After about twenty minutes, and almost running my tank dry, we slowly ascended to the top of the water. As I hit the surface, I took the last full inhalation from my now empty tank. We found to our dismay that our boat was rapidly disappearing into the blue of the horizon.

Sometime later, cold and thoroughly tired from treading water, whistling, shouting and with a soggy flag, we were feeling just a little panic setting in as we wondered what to do next. Luckily for us, a man in a speedboat, who just happened to be looking for his own lost divers, approached us and offered us a lift. I can't tell you how good it felt to haul my arse into that small boat. But you can bet our faces were a picture when we finally arrived back at our own boat. With us safely back on board, Ahmed our dive guide was in tears as he explained that he had miscounted our group and thought we were already on board. The guys who we had informed of our intentions noticed that we were nowhere to be found on board. They immediately turned the boat around, heading back towards the reef, when they saw the speed-boat approaching, with us on board. I think our little adventure would make a good film, although I believe it's been done already.

East, west, the Red Sea's the best

In all the years we've been diving, we've come to the conclusion that the best dive sites are the ones we have experienced in the Red Sea of Egypt. We try to go there at least twice a year, and it's becoming more like a second home to us. The Red Sea feels like a warm bath, especially near the top of the reefs, where temperatures can be in excess of 29 degrees and visibility can exceed sixty metres. With so much to see, you are bound to find something you overlooked on your previous dives, especially if you regularly dive the larger wrecks. As well as their histories, they can be truly extraordinary and enlightening experiences.

The warm waters around the reefs hold some of the most spectacular hard and soft corals, and an abundance of unusual flora and fauna. Some curl up the instant you approach them, whilst others simply retreat back into their stems, only to re-appear moments later like magic. There is a phenomenal abundance of sea life, the likes of which you would not see anywhere else, and so close to home. They range from the miniscule up to the bigger pelagic, and the list is endless. So I'll describe some of the ones you are more likely to see and some of their amazing habits.

A good dive guide will generally point out some of the smaller molluscs and crustaceans that are quite hard to see, like the almost invisible shrimps. Shrimps will scavenge under your fingernails for any debris and loose skin if you hang about long enough. One of my favourite creatures is the exotic-looking nudibranchs, or sea slugs. Some are no bigger than your fingernail, and so diverse in colour that they simply take your breath away watching them as they amble along on their hairy toes. Just as unusual and no less fascinating, is the aptly named Spanish Dancer. It has the amazing ability to swim upright with a graceful undulation of its mantle margins, looking for the entire world like a Spanish dancer swirling its blood red skirt. The mischievous little Sergeant Major seems to like nothing better that to protect the reef in its hordes. As the name suggests, it has black stripes on a white body and can sometimes be a little too aggressive for my liking, especially when it pulls my hair if I get too close to his reef! Some dive guides will point out the orange and white anemone fish that's more commonly known as the cartoon character, Nemo. They are very protective of their anemone habitat and tend to live in pairs or in family groups. The Bannerfish on first encounter is a strange but beautiful fish, its elongated dorsal fin curves over his back, behind what looks like a snubbed nose with pursed lips. To me, it looks from the side as though you could pick it up, like an old-fashioned flat-iron. The more conspicuous Yellow Masked Butterflyfish has a similar snub-nose shaped mouth, with which it feeds on the hard and soft coral polyps; and they are usually encountered in pairs or groups, resting under table coral. The larger Bat Fish often greet you at every bend, where they seem to hang out in large groups, seemingly strung together like a giant motionless cot-mobile over a baby's crib. I'm totally mesmerised by their big, swivelling, unblinking, doe eyes as they watch our every move. Another fish that springs to mind, the Parrot Fish, comes in a rainbow of beautiful colours and bears a striking resemblance to its namesake. It gnaws at the coral with its parrot shaped beak, while constantly evacuating sand-bombs over everything and anything that passes underneath it. Another unusual looking fish is the Cornet Fish that has large beady eyes set back along a thin flute-like body. I've nicknamed it the Jacuzzi-floozy, because it's constantly seen following the trickles of bubbles left by the pillar post on top of your air cylinder. An even funnier sight is when it perches itself at the back of your head as if it's hitching a ride amongst the constant stream released from the ventilation hole in your hood. Another fish worthy of a mention is the Titan Triggerfish. It's not a good idea to approach it when it's guarding the nursery, as it would not hesitate to attack you with a painful bite. But on the other hand, they can be really friendly – as we found out when on holiday in the Maldives, when one used to visit the bay each morning and gently eat its breakfast from the flat of your hand. But I would not advocate trying this at any time, as you could lose a finger in the process. When not hunting, the big-eyed Trevally has a look in its beady eye that seems to penetrate right through you and into your soul. Its schooling formations attract divers and snorkelers alike, as they spiral out in the blue. The most common species of Sweetlips have fat, white lips, reminiscent of the Black and White Minstrels, dressed in yellow and white striped pyjamas. They hide in groups under coral ledges during the day, and are most impressive when they swiftly pass by in their hordes. And then there's the fearsome-looking Barracuda that swims overhead perhaps just a little too close for comfort. It swims in long formation, with its ugly jutting jaw full of menacing, mirror etched teeth, not unlike those of the James Bond character, 'Jaws' that glint in the sun's rays where they cut through the crystal clear water just before dusk. The Turtle regularly scavenges the reef, and with a little bit of patience and good luck, you can entice them to feed from your hand – especially if you offer them their most favourite food, a tasty morsel of jelly fish.

Another quite common, but no less interesting sight is that of the enormous Napoleon Wrasse. It slowly sails by, with a stunning, emerald green velvety smooth body, large swivelling kindly eyes etched into a head that seems cursed with a prominent hump-shaped forehead, reminiscent of Napoleon Bonaparte's hat. It appears intelligent and aware and it is rumoured, like a dog it will nudge you if it wonts to be stroked. A rare sighting is the Sun Fish, which actually looks like a sun as it slowly swims by. It has a flat, slim-line coin-shaped body with spreading rays that look like carved wood etched around a large face on either side of his body. These have the effect of making it virtually disappear if you approach it from the front as it swims towards you. Then there is the occasional glimpse of some of the bigger pelagic, like the Manta Ray, who can change direction with just the flip of its wing. Or the White Tip Reef shark, that darts back and forth and occasionally in-between us.

Once, Barry and I saw a rare sight a very large Leopard shark sleeping behind a rock, but no-one believed us when we pointed it out.

Another rare sight is that of the Dugong – better known as Manatee, or Sea Cow. It can be seen swimming on its own, or as a family unit, feeding in the long grasses, with a couple of aunties on nanny-duty in tow. When the kids were younger we stayed at Sunset Cove off the Florida Keys, and were fortunate enough to be able to feed a large family of them with lettuce leaves. If you are extremely lucky, you might also come across one of my all-time favourites – the tiny, fragile-looking seahorse. Almost transparent, they are virtually invisible and have large woeful eyes looking out of a beautiful horse-shaped head, and a long fragile body that curls in a tail with which they anchor to the long grasses. I have read that they live as monogamous pairs and they greet each other every morning with a special ritual dance. I once I had the good fortune to hold one, and looked on in utter amazement as it curled its long, delicate tail around my little finger.

Dolphins

One of the most amazing things I have ever had the good fortune to witness was an encounter with a large pod of dolphins. I can't be precise, but there were between eight hundred and a thousand of them, riding the wake in between ours and twenty or more boats. With lightning speed, they darted in and out with such grace and agility as we cruised at full throttle, tooting our horns in all the excitement. Finally, there were hundreds of them in a great mass, as we slowly reduced speed to encircle them. When we had all come to a standstill, with fins flying in every direction, they started to perform some of the most spectacular of somersaults. Then, as if by magic, without a word being spoken, every man, woman and available crew member jumped into this heaving mass, to swim in this colossal dolphin 'soup' Unfortunately, before I could get my camera focussed in all the excitement, they disappeared back into the surf as quickly as they had come, leaving behind another great sight to behold – a vast sea of human heads left in eerie silence, just bobbing about in the frothy blue sea.

I've heard that it is not uncommon for large shoals of dolphin to out-run the boats, and I've seen that happen many times before but in rather smaller numbers. You often see them swimming in your wake while cruising through the National Parks and you might also get a glimpse of a mother in a nursery environment feeding her young. But it is quite a rare sight to see such a large pod, let alone get the once in a lifetime chance to actually swim with so many, which we were fortunately able to do.

Return to the Maldives

I've heard it said that it takes a good diver to admit defeat, and though it pains me to say it, and as sad as it might seem to some of my dive buddies, I have made the decision to hang up my fins. Certainly in the cold waters of the English coast, anyway! I have come to the conclusion that my time as a diver is nearing its end, as I feel I no longer have the strength or what it takes for some of the more challenging dives. Even though you would not notice anything amiss by just looking at me in or out of the water, the degenerative back disease that runs in the family has taken its toll and is dampening my enthusiasm in the process. It has made me think that I would not even be able to dive in the Maldives due to the strong currents, especially as after the last trip to the Red Sea in November, both myself and Mike, suffered periods of excruciating back pain.

Fortunately our last trip to the Maldives in 2012 came up before some of these problems became too serious. So the celebration of our imminent 40th Wedding Anniversary saw us in late January that year in the Equatorial Channel of the Indian Ocean in a place called Gan, the Addu Atoll far south of the Equator. We didn't think we could afford such an extravagance, due to the renovation project we had undertaken around our home at that time. But I'm glad to say that everything worked out fine in the end!

Colin, a friend and dive buddy, organised the trip of a lifetime for us, fuelling our imaginations with his constant show of enthusiasm. But it still took a lot of determination on my part, as well as a strong resolve to keep up the new fitness regime I'd set myself. And thankfully, all the determination, strength of will and hard work paid off. Because it turned out to be one of the best and most extraordinary holidays we've ever had. In fact, it also turned out to be one off my 'bucket list' to go diving with a whale shark fulfilled a life-long ambition for us both. Plus we saw hundreds of reef sharks and dozens of Manta Rays into the bargain, as had been promised.

It was an incredibly long journey, three planes and a couple of stopovers, the first in Dubai we only waited for three hours. The second stop at Male we sat in the outside café drinking beer for a couple of hours before being weighed with our bags, and aloud to board the light aircraft for the final part of our journey.
It was a little easier on the way home for which we thanked God for the rest in-between flights. In Male we lay on sun-beds around the hotel pool, where we enjoyed a nice meal and a couple of beers, sheltered from the elements in the pretty gardens totally oblivious to the wash left by the cruise ships that passed on the horizon in the sea beyond, and at the second stopover in Dubai, we rested most of the night on sumptuous sofas in the Emirates lounge bar for the princely sum of about twenty pounds, which included breakfast from an open buffet and as much drink or alcohol as you wanted.

Finally, after some thirty-two hours later, in relatively good spirits, we touched down on the last leg of our journey in an airport north of the Equator, with the strange-sounding name Hooverdoo.

On arrival we were greeted by Lisa, a small, thin bleached blond in her late thirties, and one half of the dive team couple who were looking after us for the duration of our stay. Lisa, who's also an underwater camera enthusiast, slowly walked us down to the sea-front via a lovely sandy, palm lined grove, to the moorings of a small tender. This we would use for all our forthcoming diving trips. We caught our first real glimpse of the Sea Queen, anchored just off shore, which was to be our 'home' for the next fortnight. Once on board, we were greeted by a short, stocky guy in his early forties, with dark hair and matching designer beard. He immediately shook our hands and introduced himself as Lisa's husband, Dave – the other half of the dive guide team and head honcho and chief bottle washer!

Ian and his son Liam, a couple of the club members who had made their own way there a couple of weeks prior to us, didn't seem in the least bit interested in the fact that we had arrived at long last. We sensed…something…straight away as we boarded with a little apprehension. They continued to lounge about on the upper deck, making no attempt to greet us, as we would have expected. Then we found to our dismay that the way through to the lounge had been blocked by a large bucket full of cold water, with a dozen or more water pistols floating around in it. Before we began to realise that it was all a ruse, we were caught in a well-planned ambush and bombarded with cold water bombs. The first hit Barry, our Club Chairman, right on top of his head, soaking his shirt in the process as I looked on with a grimace that probably said, 'I'm glad that wasn't me!' Then packing my pockets with some of the water pistols, I gingerly made my way up the ladder, as a couple of bombs hit home behind me, thoroughly soaking some of the others. They didn't seem to be that amused, but huddled together in the corner like a bunch of scolded Girl Guides. With some misgivings, I continued to edge up the ladder, and as I peered over the top of the sundeck, a missile came at me out of nowhere. It smacked me clean in the face, nearly knocking me off the ladder with its sheer force and leaving me hanging like a rag doll, soaked and bedraggled. When they had run out of ammunition they resorted to pistol power, fighting their way down the ladder and proceeding to chase us all around the lower deck. We fought back until eventually we all ran out of water. As I laughed, it dawned on me that the whole experience had been quite a refreshing relief from the heat of the day, and a good way to cool us down after our long, arduous journey.

Later that evening, after we had eaten dinner al fresco style around a big dining table on the front deck of the boat, we were trying to decide whether to end the evening just sitting under the stars talking, to play cards or simply go inside to watch a film. But unbeknown to us, Liam had secured another couple of loaded water pistols around the underside of the table. As we rose from the table to go inside, out of nowhere came another soaking, and another dance around the boat's perimeter water dodging. Finally, we decided that 'enough was enough' and we all went to bed.

Tired, and quite literally washed out, I flopped down on my bunk in a state of mild exhaustion, and with a wry smile I thought to myself that maybe it did not fare well with everyone, but I for one thought it was a brilliant welcome! But I hasten to say it did not stop there, in fact it was just the start.

The Northern Atoll, The Villingili Kanda Reef

The next morning, we dived around the Northern Atoll. We made our usual dive checks at the surface, i.e. our weights are heavy enough to take us just below the surface and to resurface with ease. You are obliged to do this on your first day's diving. We use the acronym B.A.R. for our body check before a dive. B is for Buoyancy, meaning the direct feed is attached, air dumps are working, and you have your weight belt on. A is for Air, which is ensuring that it's fully flowing through your mouthpiece and dump valves, including your octopus rig. R is for Release, which means you know where and how your buddy's buckles and belts work. These checks are done before every dive, to ensure that you have not forgotten anything. This regime is supposed to cut down on the times and the hassle of having to swim back to the boat for more weight or for something you have forgotten. But you would be surprised how often this actually happens throughout the week, even with the most experienced of divers – there's always someone who's forgotten something or other, i.e. their camera or their torch, or they've just forgotten one of the most important things – their weight belt. This can present a problem when we need to get down quite quickly, as you can find yourself being pulled along at a rapid pace away from the reef if there is a strong current on the surface. Back on the boat after the dive that morning, I felt quite nauseous due to the swell of the water, and whilst stripping off my dive gear, to my horror I discovered that my feet had turned a bright shade of orange. Try as I might, the colour would not wash off. There was much debate about how my boots must have been contaminated prior to the dive, with maybe something at home that had got into the wash. But I managed to brush off the endless leg pulling, laughter and comments with a wry smile.

The next morning we had a great dive on the Villingili Kanda reef where we saw both a White Tip and a Nurse Shark asleep under some rocks. Back on board after the dive, both Mike and I discovered to our horror that the dyed-foot-phantom had struck again. This time I was not alone – he had caught us both out and we both had a pair of even harder to wash off indigo blue feet.

Lisa and John, who also executed the every-day running of the boat, woke us at about five the following morning to go snorkelling with hordes of Mobular Rays, and the absolute highlight of our holiday, the appearance of a six-metre baby Whale Shark. This was an experience that I will never forget! Evidently it was drawn by the swirling, foggy plankton soup, caught up in the brightness of the lights which John had strategically placed either side of the rear of the boat.

Unfortunately, that morning Mike had a bad pain in his ear, and had abandoned the snorkelling. He said he could feel the plankton biting the inside of his ear, and he could blow air out through it when he tried to equalise. So we concluded that he must have a small perforation, and it was decided that it would be best for him to go ashore to see a doctor on one of the larger islands the next day. The doctor's equipment was so antiquated - he had just an ear trumpet to look into Mike's ear, and the language barrier seemed to cause him trouble in making a diagnosis. So he turned his attention to me. He offered an overhaul and attempted to take my blood pressure, as his nurse busied herself filling out forms behind me. I refused to sign the forms and made a quick exit. Once outside, we were very reluctant to visit the local hospital, but were informed by our guide that they work pretty much the same, if not better, than ours. So after a bit of debate about the pros and cons of the situation, Mike decided to take the plunge. To our complete surprise we found them to be far more efficient than our hospitals back home, with some very high-tech equipment. Unfortunately, the German doctor, who also seemed to have little idea as to what to do, apart from prescribing a course of antibiotic drops to administer before he went to bed and first thing in the morning, Mike was devastated when he was advised that he should not dive for the duration of the holiday, as he could easily pick up a bad infection. I found it a bit embarrassing having to sit in a plush waiting-room in my flip-flops trying to hide my strange blue feet from the many smart nursing staff in attendance.

A very strange thing happened to us on the way out of the hospital. Some of the local people obviously thought we were visiting celebrities or VIPs, as they gathered around us to look us over. A young girl gingerly made her way over to me, and made a sort of curtesy as she reached for my hand. It makes me wonder who they thought we were – probably they haven't seen many tall, blonde white women in their part of the world. It has been said that I vaguely resembled Princess Diana in my youth, but I suppose the blue blood so evident in my feet might have added to this confusion.

Since my dive buddy Mike was incapacitated at the time of our first dive, I got the chance to dive with Lisa. I must say I was totally blown away by the number of sharks we saw on the reef that day. In fact, at one point there were so many that I gave up counting. They just kept on coming, seeming to eye our every move as they swam up and down the perimeter of the reef. Then with a quick swish of their tail fin they would spin around and nonchalantly swim past us from the other direction – but a little closer each time. Mike was extremely envious when I showed him the video I'd taken on my new digital camera. It all looked so surreal as I watched some extra footage of Lisa, at about forty metres down trying to coax a giant lemon shark nearer as she filmed it lying in the sand next to her. I was totally mesmerised.

As luck would have it, one of our guys called Mike Batty came up with a mask with special earmuffs attached, to help take away the pressure on the eardrums. He said he had used it himself to protect a perforated eardrum on one of his diving trips. So when we revisited the same dive site that afternoon, Mike wore them and he was over the moon at being able to dive so soon after, and with no pain to speak of he was able to carry on for the rest of the fortnight. Just imagine for one moment going all that way, at a cost of nearly seven grand, to be told you would not be able to dive. It doesn't bear thinking about, does it?

Kuda Kandu

Throughout the week we dived some of the most spectacular reefs. Two in particular are renowned for their Manta Ray feeding stations. And we were very lucky to have dived them both a couple of times each. One was called Mudukan and the other Kuda Kandu. Even though the strong current was horrendous most of the time, we managed pretty well without incident, and it was well worth all the effort. We anchored ourselves down by whatever means were available on the reef, and tucked down behind giant boulders or wedged between a couple of smaller ones. Mike found his own unique way by lying down and digging in his heels. It did prove a little hazardous at times as he was frequently turned over like a leaf in the wind, and consequently collided with anyone else who had decided to do the same.

We had been advised by Colin and some of the others at the beginning of the holiday to bring our crab hook away with us. We seemed to be the only ones who actually took this advice and it proved invaluable as we were able to hook onto the reef, leaving hands free, and I was able to take some stunning video footage of the Manta Rays there. They can grow up to 6-7 metres from wing-tip to wing-tip. We looked on awe-struck as they swam down, looping the loop, and unfurling the paddle-like cephalic lobes that projected from each side of their head. They used these to scoop up the plankton bearing water into their very broad oval mouths whilst gliding in one after the other, like planes flying low over our heads. They made it seem effortless as they glided gracefully down, in complete contrast to us humans, tossed about underneath them like sailors in a storm. Sometimes they would hover at arms-length above us, as we hung on to the reef in one of the strongest currents we have ever had to endure. One of the guys, Mike Sullivan, looking on from a few feet away, managed to get some stunning video footage showing a very large Ray swooping down as if ready to sweep up anyone who stood in its way. Its gaping jaw was so wide that we could see right down its throat as it paused in front of us. It took our breath clean away as it then moved and just hovered overhead, seemingly enjoying the residual air bubbles that skimmed its giant frame. We reached up to try to stroke the enormous underbelly that spread out over us like a giant white umbrella covered in the pattern of black spots unique to each one. I know that being tossed around in the current at the bottom of the sea doesn't sound like much fun for some, who might read this, but this astonishing experience far outweighed any discomfort, and it is another experience I would not have missed for the world.

As we crossed the Equator in the Southern Hemisphere, it is customary to ring the ship's bell, to 'bring us all safely home'. This dates back to a time when sailors were very superstitious and made grovelling pleas to the God of the Sea, Neptune, with his giant trident, which he used as a sceptre to calm the sea. Initially, the celebration was largely in recognition of the Equator being crossed safely, and a significant part of the journey being over. However, over time the tradition became more of an entertainment, taking on the flavour of the period.

Whilst sunbathing on deck during the first week of the holiday, it became apparent that the phantom toe-nail painter had struck. His first victim of the week, poor old Howard Carter, was left with bright green toe-nails, who was not entirely amused by the phantom's antics. He struck again after lunch that day, and I think it was Andy Stevenson who fell victim, with a diabolical bright orange colour. All afternoon, we dared not shut our eyes for fear of being his next victim, but none-the-less, the perpetrator managed to work his way around the whole of the boat. I was left until last - I think it was because my toenails were already painted, but also because I had begun to suspect that the culprit was young Liam Mather, as I had been keeping a close eye on him. In fact, I caught him red-handed when I was sun-bathing, trying to paint my fingernails bright blue from under the chair. One of the guys, who should remain nameless, had had enough of Liam's antics, so to pay him back whilst he was asleep, egged on by the others, decided to varnish his eyebrows with a bright orange sparkly nail polish. I would add that I thought it was a bit drastic at the time, and I worried that Liam might not be able to remove it at the end of the holiday. Fortunately, he only managed to do one eyebrow before he woke up, and after being sufficiently ridiculed, he was able to remove it with some nail-polish remover. I don't think I have ever seen anyone so upset by a taste of their own medicine! Liam's dad, Ian, had to calm him down by reminding him of the old saying: 'If you can't take it, don't dish it out.'

I don't think everyone agreed with me, but all the japing around certainly made my holiday a lot more entertaining, and it was all good clean fun which made us all laugh throughout our fortnight's stay. The holiday was one that I'll never forget, not just for the stunning dives, but for the whole experience that fulfilled one of our greatest ambitions, making it the holiday of a lifetime.

Why Do I Love Diving?

Whilst a holiday in a hotel brings many social opportunities, diving can provide the best of both worlds, giving you the opportunity to see things from a completely different perspective. I can't explain the euphoria, that feeling of freedom whilst flying through the water with a bird's-eye view, or of entering a spectacular wreck, or simply just skimming along the top of a colourful reef, where gentle turtles feed, and vast shoals of Barracuda swim menacingly overhead, and where Jacks swim in ever increasing circles, and if you are really lucky a giant Manta Ray glides by, and where, out of the blue, if you are vigilant, a Reef Shark will sometimes make an appearance.

As a qualified diver, I am constantly asked by family and friends if I am ever frightened by the sea. My answer is always the same and I am assured this is an indication of a good diver, that even though I am always slightly apprehensive before most dives because of the many things you have to be aware of, I can honestly say that as soon as I get into the water all the training comes into play. I can relax in such a way that I enjoy it and am in total awe of the entire experience.

It's a great thrill to be part of a group of like-minded people, especially when we race about in a rib that's filled to capacity, yet still manages to plane across the top of the water, riding the bumps and swells as we hold on for dear life, whilst screaming with delight. Sometimes we're snug in our dry suits, oblivious to the wet and cold, and sometimes in our wetsuits with the warmth of the sun and the sea spray in our hair and faces.

Some of our most enjoyable times were spent seeking out new adventures and diving around the globe, sometimes on our own and at other times with club members. But the best times were the ones we spent with our children Michael and Zoë and eventually we all dived together and were able to show them the great wonders in the vast blue yonder.

In closing,

We bid a sad but fond farewell to our favourite live-aboard, the Sea Queen that sank on 22nd December 2013. She was sailing from the Red Sea resort of Sharm to a dry dock in the Suez, where only one survived the misfortune that struck her on her last voyage that day.

We commiserate with all the families who lost their loved ones amongst the missing crew. We will miss Reda, Hesham and our friend Bob, who we saw over the past twelve years, mature into a very pleasant and helpful young man. Also although he often seemed quiet and reserved, the delightful and sometimes boisterous Captain, Sied Dushma, who showed himself to be more than game for a laugh.

We will miss you all, with your enlivening and entertaining dance that brought us all a little closer.

And you will dwell in our hearts for a long time to come.

I hope you enjoy reading this Book as much as I enjoyed writing it.

Brenda
17-8-2017

Made in the USA
Columbia, SC
05 August 2017